Play-based Learning in the Primary School

Education at SAGE

SAGE is a leading international publisher of journals, books, and electronic media for academic, educational, and professional markets.

Our education publishing includes:

- accessible and comprehensive texts for aspiring education professionals and practitioners looking to further their careers through continuing professional development

- inspirational advice and guidance for the classroom

- authoritative state of the art reference from the leading authors in the field

Find out more at: **www.sagepub.co.uk/education**

Play-based Learning in the Primary School

Mary Briggs and Alice Hansen

Los Angeles | London | New Delhi
Singapore | Washington DC

First published 2012

SAGE Publications Ltd
1 Oliver's Yard
55 City Road
London EC1Y 1SP

SAGE Publications Inc.
2455 Teller Road
Thousand Oaks, California 91320

SAGE Publications India Pvt Ltd
B 1/I 1 Mohan Cooperative Industrial Area
Mathura Road
New Delhi 110 044

SAGE Publications Asia-Pacific Pte Ltd
3 Church Street
#10-04 Samsung Hub
Singapore 049483

Library of Congress Control Number: 2011932438

British Library Cataloguing in Publication data

A catalogue record for this book is available from the British Library

ISBN 978-0-85702-823-5
ISBN 978-0-85702-824-2 (pbk)

Typeset by C&M Digitals (P) Ltd, Chennai, India
Printed in India by Replika Press Pvt Ltd

CONTENTS

ACKNOWLEDGEMENTS

We wish to extend our sincere thanks to Cathy Styles and staff (Croftlands Junior School), Hank Williams, Sarah Lonsdale (York St John University), the McGregor Family, Victoria O'Farrell (Central Lancaster High School), Sara Bradley (Dallas Road School) and those other teachers who wish to remain anonymous for supporting the inclusion of their case studies.

ABOUT THE AUTHORS

Mary Briggs is an Associate Professor in the Institute of Education at the University of Warwick. She teaches on a number of different education courses with a specific research interest in mathematics education, leadership, assessment, and mentoring and coaching. She has worked in a wide range of settings including children's homes, special, primary school and universities.

Dr Alice Hansen is an educational consultant. Her research interests are in mathematics education, using technology to enhance learning and teaching, and curriculum development. Her main focus is continuing professional development for practitioners, teachers and other educators in early years settings, primary schools, initial teacher training providers and other educational settings in the UK and abroad.

INTRODUCTION

In the UK and many other countries around the world there are a growing number of primary schools developing their pedagogical approach to the curriculum so that the children receive a broad, balanced curriculum that encourages high achievement and engagement. The development includes the use of 'creative' and 'innovative' approaches to learning and teaching that put children and their needs at the centre. This book addresses many of the issues related to this pedagogic approach by focusing on play-based learning and teaching across the primary and elementary school.

The book begins by presenting a number of biological, societal, educational and developmental views of play. These address the social/cultural, behavioural/physical, affective/emotional and cognitive/intellectual aspects of play. We also present the 'planning paradox' in relation to play which is one of the main issues related to a play-based approach to learning and teaching. The planning paradox states that there is a tension for teachers between the desire for children to feel a play-like freedom within more formal school-based learning, but that this is unsatisfactory if the child's and teacher's agenda differ. This book addresses this significant issue.

The book centres on a number of principles of play. We know that every school context and every child's need within that context is different. Therefore we use guiding principles that work in all types of play regardless of the situation. The principles are introduced in Chapter 2 as roles for older learners. We use the premise that children have the capacity to be autonomous learners, creative learners, investigators, problem solvers, reflective learners and social learners.

Building on the earlier chapters that outline what play for older children is and the roles that older children undertake within play, Chapter 3 identifies the types of play that are suitable for 5–11-year-olds. These are:

- artistic or design play
- controlled imaginary play/social dramatic play
- exploratory play
- games play
- integrated play
- play using the whole school environment and beyond
- replication play
- small world play
- role play
- virtual play.

Play-based approaches to learning are synonymous with the early years phase of education, yet this chapter uses research to demonstrate how each type of play can effectively address older learners' needs including their academic attainment. Each type of play is illustrated with a small practical idea.

Chapter 4 draws together the principles and types of play by providing full case studies from primary schools in England where play-based approaches to learning are being utilised. It is our intention that the case studies will act as a catalyst for you to try play-based approaches in your teaching and will also ilustrate the principles and types of play outlined in earlier chapters.

The planning paradox is revisited in Chapter 5. The tension that it identifies is critically discussed, with a focus on the role of teachers and other adults in a play-based approach to learning and teaching. We look at different models for play-based learning environments and the possible roles for adults and children within these. Practical advice for involving adults and finding other adults to help is given.

In Chapter 6 we look at the issues around planning for play activities with 5–11-year-old children and how both adults and children can be involved in the planning and organisation of play environments. It includes discussion of the design and planning of environments, as well as the development of environments through spontaneous events in the classroom and outside as a response to children's interests and their ideas. This chapter raises questions about how we stimulate play with older learners and how we allow the element of choice within activities for the children.

In a play-based approach to learning and teaching, assessment methods and strategies are different to the more traditional approaches often used. In Chapter 7 we address a number of significant issues that teachers often face in relation to assessing during a play-based approach. Aspects such as process vs. product, output vs. outcomes, and hard vs. soft outcomes are considered. We challenge existing widespread practice to ask who can undertake the assessment and look at the role children have in assessing their own achievements.

We also look at a range of assessment methods that move away from traditional paper-based evidence and encourage you to try some of them. We take observation, a key assessment strategy used in the early years, and consider its application in settings for older children. Finally, we consider reporting assessment findings to parents.

Inclusion is the availability of opportunity for *all* learners to make progress learn from activities through the removal of any barriers to learning and development. These may be physical, emotional, social, cultural, religious or cognitive. In Chapter 8 we consider how all children can be offered a rich and enjoyable experience that will support their development in the widest sense. We use speaking and listening as a tool for being a reflective and social learner. We look at issues that are more particular to children who have English as an additional language and more widely the social issues that impact on all members of a school community.

Finally, Chapter 9 discusses how play-based approaches to learning and teaching can support children's transition from primary to secondary schooling. It provides a case study of how a primary and secondary school collaborate with a view to supporting the learners in both settings in a range of transitions (for example, from primary to secondary school and from secondary school into a career). Issues about using a skills-based curriculum, the impact of children's levels of confidence on ease of transition, and links between primary and secondary school experiences are explored.

Overall the book supports teachers and trainee teachers in thinking about why and how a play-based approach to learning is effective in the whole primary school. It considers a wide range of school contexts, and offers innovative and practical advice for how a play-based approach to learning can be implemented as a school-wide approach or in a single classroom.

CHAPTER 1

WHAT IS PLAY IN THE PRIMARY OR ELEMENTARY SCHOOL?

Introduction

It is widely accepted within educational literature that play is a difficult notion to define.

> Play is a complex phenomenon that occurs naturally for most children; they move through the various stages of play development and are able to add complexity, imagination, and creativity to their thought processes and actions. (Mastrangelo, 2009: 34)

Because of the nature of play, we do not offer a precise definition. Instead, in this chapter we present a range of views of play, including biological, historical, societal, educational and developmental in order to support you to develop your own understanding of play in the primary school.

 Points for reflection

Before reading on, think about the play that you engaged with as a child and adolescent, and engage with now as an adult. As you read each section below, reflect on how your own play could be seen from a biological, historical, societal, educational and developmental view.

Biological views of play

Much research identifies that play is a necessary condition for some birds, reptiles, and all mammals including high-order animals such as primates (see, for example, Elkonin, 2005; Oliveira et al., 2010; Palagi et al., 2004; Liu, 2008). It appears to be generally accepted that, from a biological perspective, play is imitative in nature and is a necessary condition for survival in the species. For example, play fighting is observed in rodents (Pellis and Iwaniuk, 2004) and for primates, social play and grooming encourage extended periods of social cohesion (Palagi et al. 2004). Birds also exhibit social behaviour in play, from chasing to reciprocal object play (Diamond and Bond, 2003). Although play is mostly observed in the young of animal species, play is present in adulthood too (Palagi et al., 2006).

From this literature it is possible to conclude that for animals 'play behaviour is far from ... a purposeless activity' (Palagi et al., 2004: 949), but is this the case for humans? Craine (2010) seems to think it must be. He explains how children in very challenging circumstances (such as waiting in emergency hospital rooms, living during the Holocaust, or living in ghettos) play spontaneously and uncontrollably. They often have little to play with and face pain, hunger or uncertainty, yet they use whatever they have to play creatively. He proposes that this desire to play may be an innate part of being human. Other animals only play if they are happy and fulfilled (Palagi et al., 2004), yet Craine suggests otherwise for humans. Therefore, if playing is such a strong innate human response, how has society's and education's view of it developed through history?

Historical views of play

Societal views of play

Play is an issue that has been explored by many writers over the previous two centuries who have established alternative perspectives on its role and usefulness. There are writers who have seen play as not holding any real value but purely as a means of using up children's excess energy, for example, Spencer in 1898. Therefore play from such perspectives was not seen as a medium for learning. Others, such as Groos (1890), decided that play allowed children to prepare for life by providing opportunities for the practice of skills and offering the possibility of exploring ways of learning what they will need to know as adults, though having potential excess energy to burn in engaging in the activities was an advantage but not a necessity. For those like Hall (1908) looking at play from an anthropological perspective, play allows children to act out all the primitive behaviours of our evolutionary past, for example, play fighting is reminiscent of the wrestling activities highly visible in past societies and cultures. These writers clearly see play as associated with learning but very specific kinds of knowledge is being learnt. The focus is on practising existing knowledge within society which is linked to cultural heritage and roles within occupations. It could be argued that his view of play is stagnating in our changing society where the skills and knowledge are shifting and we do not necessarily need the existing skill sets that children can learn from watching adults at work or in roles in the home. Those following the principles of Maria Montessori would still see this practice of the skills of everyday life as important, not only for practical life but also to help children develop the concentration and co-ordination of mind and body. This view of learning continues to be popular across the world.

Educational views of play

The impact of the National Curriculum

In primary school the place of play has shifted over time from the 1960s and 70s. This was influenced by Plowden (CACE, 1967) and during that time experiential learning environments could be seen in all classes up to and including Year 6. This continued into the 1980s before the introduction of the National Curriculum in 1989, when there was a move away from projects or thematic approaches to curriculum planning. The next three decades saw the rise of subjects as the dominant approach for organising learning. The 1990s and first decade of the new century were dominated by the National Strategy's approaches to planning, teaching and learning.

Perhaps it is the way we conceptualise learning that is part of the problem. We are bounded by notions of curriculum which stem from the separation of subjects and learning into compartments both in time and space. Teachers often struggle to make the connections between these artificial separations and as a consequence learners make their own arbitrary connections which can lead to the establishment of misconceptions and lack of understanding.

> Learning and teaching are often assumed to 'take place' in particular slots of a timetable in particular classrooms associated with particular curriculum subjects. (Loveless and Thacker, 2005: 4)

The need to demonstrate results of policies and a nostalgic view of a past education system that worked because of its traditional methods and rigour has led to politicians appearing to be austere. This is demonstrated in the following extract, which suggests that children are in schools to work and not to have fun.

> Ministers have presided over the death of fun and play in the primary school curriculum, according to the results of an inquiry published today. (Garner, 2007)

However, there were significant consequences across primary schools of moving away from play-based activities. Christine Gilbert, the chair of the Teaching and Learning in 2020 Review Group, stated that 'too many children drift into underachievement and disengagement and fail to make progress in their learning' (2006: 12).

This is a particularly saddening indictment of the state of education at the beginning of the 21st Century by Christine Gilbert, who became Her Majesty's Chief Inspector of Schools in that same year. After all, children start in education with an enthusiasm for learning through their natural curiosity about the world around them. They are keen to learn with inquisitive minds, yet the system appears to force them into learning the skills, knowledge and especially the facts that will help them to pass the assessments, particularly the exams, in order to make the grade. Our education system appears to have failed many children for whom learning is no longer a fun activity but a tedious means to an end.

Making amends

The introduction of *Excellence and Enjoyment* (DfE, 2003) began the reversal of the subject-led trend and reintroduced notions of cross-curricular links and aspects of creativity. Alongside this the personalised learning agenda was introduced to try to address disaffection and lack of engagement. Schools worked with these changes in different ways. One Bristol school which implemented a creative curriculum found that giving their learners greater choice in their curriculum:

- raised children's motivation levels, in particular for home learning;
- helped children become more engaged with their learning in lessons; and
- enhanced teachers' motivation by encouraging them to get to grips with completely new 'topics'. (Haydon, 2008)

Developmental views of play and learning

This book positions play activities within a new paradigm for the future for learners in the primary school. This paradigm is introduced in Chapter 2. However, there is an extensive literature which includes writers viewing play in different ways and it is useful to review a few of the works of authors who have explicitly linked play to learning in different ways.

In summary, the majority of these writers see play as a vehicle for learning whether that be the therapeutic, practising of existing skills or developing symbolic thinking. See Table 1.1.

Among a majority of contemporary researchers, writers and commentators it is widely accepted that play is essential for younger children's learning, yet as children get older there is a shift in the emphasis given to play. Views differ about the role of play around the age group on which it should be focused; for example, Strandell sees play as

an activity that separates children from the real, adult world. It has become one of the expressions for the banishment of children to the margins of society. Play has become an expression of a kind of activity that has no place in real society; something easy that children engage in while waiting for entrance into society.
(2000: 147)

Play is sometimes seen as something special for children as they are different from adults. As a consequence play, according to Pellegrini and Boyd, has become 'an almost hallowed concept for teachers of young children' (1993: 105). For Ailwood (2003) there are three dominant discourses of play which she identifies as:

1   *A romantic/nostalgic discourse*. Ailwood suggests that the romantic/nostalgic discourse attempts to look back to a time when children had more freedom to play outside without adult intervention. There is a view that all children had access to this kind of environment whereas the reality is that this was not uniformly available. This view of play is also based within the dominance of Western culture where play is highly valued for children's emotional well-being. This is supported by the work discussed above where play is seen as something all adults have enjoyed and is viewed through rose-coloured glasses as idyllic. What this discourse fails to recognise are the difficult issues that children encounter when playing, such as lack of friends, disagreements with friends, bullying, issues surrounding toys and sharing or just having nowhere to play.

2   A *play characteristic discourse* which is linked to the first discourse and despite some variations in practice is commonly taken as the starting point for many writers about children's play. These characteristics have some consistencies in their description but one of the most well known comes from Tina Bruce:

> *The 12 features of play*
>
> 1   Using first-hand experiences
> 2   Making up rules
> 3   Making props
> 4   Choosing to play
> 5   Rehearsing the future
> 6   Pretending
> 7   Playing alone
> 8   Playing together
> 9   Having a personal agenda
> 10 Being deeply involved
> 11 Trying out recent learning
> 12 Co-ordinating ideas, feelings and relationships for free flow play. (2001: 117)

3   A *developmental discourse* (Ailwood, 2003: 288) which is linked to cognitive psychology and focuses on Piaget and Vygotskian views of learning outlined in Table 1.1. This is promoted through children having opportunities for dialogues about their learning which are available in 'play situations'.

> A child's play is not simply a reproduction of what he has experienced, but a creative reworking of the impressions he has acquired. (Vygotsky, 2004: 11)

For Vygotsky play provides an important context for learning and development: 'Only theories maintaining that a child does not have to satisfy the basic requirements of life, but can live in search of pleasure, could possibly suggest that a child's world is a play world' (1933: 1). But: 'The child moves forward essentially through play activity. Only in this sense can play be termed a leading activity that determines the child's development.' Of key importance here is the dialogue through which children can articulate their developing ideas and adults can interact to navigate them through the mine field of potential misconceptions and social interaction issues.

Table 1.1 Overview of key theorists and their views of learning and play

Key theorist	View of learning	View of play
Freud (1975); Erikson (1950); Winnicott (1971); Issacs (1929)	Psychoanalytic perspective	Play is a cathartic experience for children enabling the emotional and cognitive growth of children in a safe environment.
Piaget (1999); Bruner et al. (1976)	Constructivist perspective	Play is a product of assimilation. During play, children practise skills to move towards mastery and try out new combinations of behaviour in a safe setting. High value play leads to intellectual development.
Vygotsky (1978)	Social cultural perspective	Play is a vehicle for social interaction and is the leading source of development in the pre-school years. Play develops symbolic thinking by facilitating the separation of thought from objects and actions. Vygotsky questioned whether or not the child is truly free in play, as the play situation actually sets the limits on behaviour. Through language and symbolic thought, play involves self-regulatory behaviour that involves children developing the ability to plan, monitor and reflect upon their own behaviour.

Play as a precursor to formal learning

Most writers see play as making the transition to more structured learning. In this extract from Siraj-Blatchford's (2009) table of a model of pedagogic progression in play the final category focuses on this transition rather than seeing play as a continuous part of lifelong learning.

Table 1.2 Play as a transition to formal learning (Siraj-Blatchford, 2009: 82)

Playful activity	Sustained shared thinking	Pedagogy	Learning	Development potential
Transition to learning activity	Collaboration in increasingly structured activities and games with more complex rules	Encouragement of extended play (over days) to promote self regulation, planning and memory. Progressive reduction of scaffolding in planning. Scaffolding more disciplined collaborations, e.g. carrying out an 'investigation'	Reflection upon the relationship between 'pretend' signs and 'real' meanings. Orientation towards more formal learning and school Learning to learn	Towards learning to learn and the development of learning 'dispositions'

For older children curriculum objectives normally take precedence and traditionally learning is seen as a structured activity controlled by the teacher. Again this is highlighted in the extract from Table 1.2. The expected learning outcomes for older children are raised with a heavy emphasis on progress. While it is appropriate to have high expectations of children's learning and progress there is a tendency to make this type of learning routine and formulaic. For young children play is seen as a means of exploring and making sense of their environment. There is a real sense of wonder if you watch young children discovering as they explore, for example, the first time a child finds a woodlouse that will curl into a ball when touched, or a magnet attracts something metallic, or a jack in a box pops out from its box. There are so many examples of the joy of discovery that we have all witnessed with young children. Underlying this perspective is the idea that as learners we move on from 'play' to a different kind of learning with different rules and purposes.

Play for life

Others, however, see play existing throughout life – albeit manifested in different ways, depending on age, maturation, context and experience. Ortlieb explains, for example, that 'children explore their environments, adolescents engage in athletic competitions, and adults travel on vacations in hopes of experiencing the "new"' (2010: 241).

Indeed, Bergen and Williams (2008) demonstrated that when young adults were asked to recall their most salient play experiences, they tended to provide very detailed and happy memories from the age of 8–12 years.

The section below presents a set of developmental stages of play that can be seen across the primary school and beyond.

The domains of developmental stages of play

Canning reminds us that adults tend to look for the outcomes of play, rather than the 'complex processes that are happening within play' (2007: 233) and this section strives to address this issue.

There is much early years-related literature that demonstrates how play is developmentally appropriate for young children. For example,

> Play-based advocates ... believe that young children's thinking and learning is qualitatively different from that of adults. For this reason, it requires a curriculum that is commensurate with their age and developmental status. (Walsh et al. 2006: 202)

While we agree that there is a specific play-related approach to learning necessary in the early years, we wish to argue that play – in its widest sense – is appropriate for humans of *any* age. Bodrova and Leong (1996) identify three stages of play that they loosely equate to Piaget's development stages:

- Stage 1: Practice or functional play (generally observed during sensorimotor period)
- Stage 2: Symbolic play (emerges during preoperational period)
- Stage 3: Games with rules (peaks during concrete operational period).

More specifically, Liu (2008) defines the developmental stages of play in relation to the following domains:

- behavioural/physical domain (the physical well-being and motor skills)
- affective/emotional domain
- cognitive/intellectual domain (language and thought)
- social/cultural domain.

Guided by Liu's domains we have identified examples in the literature of how play develops during the primary years in these domains. While the Early Years Foundation Stage (EYFS) literature is very rich, research and its associated literature in relation to the older primary stage is sparse but growing in quantity. We intentionally choose not to identify particular age-stage-related development as Bodrova and Leong have done because, as later chapters will show, children demonstrate various behaviours and developmental outcomes in different play situations.

Although we present Table 1.3 discretely, it is important to remember that in the primary school, each of the domains are interrelated. For example, 'emotional and social development are linked because children's social interactions are usually emotionally charged' (Ashiabi, 2007: 200).

Table 1.3 The developmental domains of play

Domain	Development of domain
Social/cultural	• Natural functions become cultural functions through one's ability to self-regulate and master them. • Infants expect reciprocity in social interaction with adults. There is little or no interaction between children. This develops into children being able to take on others' perspectives and co-ordinating roles. (Fromberg, 2002; Kravtsov and Kravtsova, 2010)
Behavioural/ physical	• Children initiate their own play (e.g. shaking shakers), and later physical prowess becomes more refined. • Earlier, children express themselves in absolute terms (e.g. 'I am a good boy'). Later, children begin to describe themselves in more mixed ways, dependent on the context. • Earlier, children express their own points of view. Later, children perceive and respond to the goals, perceptions and beliefs of others. (Ensink and Mayes, 2010; Fromberg, 2002; Landry et al., 2009; Zhang et al., 2010)
Affective/ emotional	• Early on, children develop a sense of what they like and dislike to understand self. Having power in play provides children with the opportunity to develop emotionally. • Primary aged children develop a general ability to know what others may be thinking and imagine what they may be feeling. They increasingly think about themselves in terms of their behaviour, performance and interpersonal relationships. • Earlier, children turn to adults to regulate emotion. Later, self-regulation of emotion, takes the form of responsibility by the child. (Ashiabi, 2007; Canning, 2007)
Cognitive/ intellectual	• Development of self-regulated learning includes children being able to select from a repertoire of strategies and monitor their progress in using these strategies. • Play themes become more coherent and play episodes are more extended. • Language becomes more complex as the domain develops. • Earlier, there is the emergence of intentionality, then children begin to understand when a false statement is being made. Finally, the development of understanding of others' intentions in everyday communication is achieved. (Ensink and Mayes, 2010; Fromberg, 2002; Nutbrown and Clough, 2009)

Play and the 'planning paradox'

We conclude this chapter by acknowledging a particular tension (the 'planning paradox') about play in primary schools:

> Play can facilitate learning and so there is a desire to incorporate play-like freedom into more formal school-based learning, even for older pupils. However, such a strategy transfers control over what is learned away from the teacher to the pupils themselves. This is unsatisfactory if the teacher has an agenda in which certain specific knowledge should be assimilated. (Ainley et al., 2006: 23)

There is clearly a need to explore different approaches for specific groups in primary education, for example the focus on a 'dangerous books culture for boys' discussed by Gove (2010) in the *Sunday Times* after a BBC programme led by Gareth Malone introducing boys to physical challenges. While it can be easy to offer children new and novel experiences as a one-off series of sessions outside the school constraints, this can make it appear that there are simple answers to engaging learners. What is possible for a celebrity who is not bound by the rules with which most teachers work is not necessarily the immediate answer for all schools. However, within programmes like this there are elements that can easily be taken on by teachers including the use of physical activities, challenges and competition for boys. Play-based curricula are one way that teachers offer this to specific groups within their classes.

This paradox is particularly evident in primary schools in relation to accountability through the inspection and assessment procedures as the following quote for the Cambridge review of primary education shows.

> The problem of the curriculum is inseparable from the problem of assessment and testing. Unless the national assessment system is reformed, especially at KS2, changes to the curriculum will have limited impact and the curriculum outside the favoured zone of tested subjects will continue to be compromised. (Alexander et al., 2009: 3)

However, this book offers a way forward to address the issues that have been raised in this chapter. We present case studies where teachers and student teachers have taken risks in schools which are identified as 'outstanding' in Ofsted terms or in schools whose performance shows their pedagogy achieves results in national testing. Therefore we present a solution to the planning paradox – a play-based approach to learning and teaching across the primary school.

 Summary

This book focuses on what play in the primary school may look like and this chapter has introduced a number of ways of conceptualising play: biological, historical, societal, educational and developmental. Within the latter, play has been considered through the domains of social/cultural behavioural/physical, affective/emotional and cognitive/intellectual development. Because we know that all children develop in different ways and at different times depending on the context, we have not identified ages and stages of development within these domains. However, the literature shows us that they are evident throughout the primary school. The 'planning paradox' states that there is a tension between a motivating, child-led curriculum and an objectives-based, teacher-led curriculum.

Reflect upon your own practice by thinking about the following questions in relation to play activities.

1 Has your perspective on play changed after reading this chapter?
2 What are the views of colleagues teaching across primary/elementary education on play?
3 What do you think society's views, including those of parents, would be on play for older children?
4 How might teaching and learning in your classroom change with more play-based activities?
5 What, at this stage, do you think would be the bigger challenges to shifting practice?

This chapter has set the scene for the remainder of this book, which continues to illustrate what play in the primary school looks like and offers a way forward to address the play and the 'planning paradox' issue commonly seen in primary schools today.

Further reading

Alexander, R., Armstrong, M., Flutter, J., Hargreaves, L., Harrison, D., Harlen, W., Hartley-Brewer, E., Kershner, R., Macbeath, J., Mavall, B., Northen, S., Pugh, G. and Utting, D. (2009) *Children, their World, their Education: Final Report and Recommendations of the Cambridge Primary Review*. London: Routledge.

Bruce, T. (2001) *Learning Through Play: Babies, Toddlers and the Foundation Years*. London: Hodder and Stoughton.

Bruner, J.S., Jolly, A., and Sylva, K. (1976) *Play: Its Role in Development and Evolution*. New York: Basic Books.

Vygotsky, L. (1933) *Play and its Role in the Mental Development of the Child*. Cambridge, MA: Voprosy.

References

Ailwood, J. (2003) 'Governing Early Childhood Education through Play', *Contemporary Issues in Early Childhood*, 4 (3): 286–99.

Ainley, J. Pratt, D. and Hansen, A. (2006) 'Connecting engagement and focus in pedagogic task design', *British Educational Research Journal*, 32 (1): 23–38.

Alexander, R., Armstrong, M., Flutter, J., Hargreaves, L., Harrison, D., Harlen, W., Hartley-Brewer, E., Kershner, R., Macbeath, J., Mavall, B., Northen, S., Pugh, G. and Utting, D. (2009) *Children, their World, their Education: Final Report and Recommendations of the Cambridge Primary Review*. London: Routledge.

Ashiabi, G. (2007) 'Play in the preschool classroom: its socioemotional significance and the teacher's role in play', *Early Childhood Education Journal*, 35 (2): 199–207.

Bergen, D. and Williams, E. (2008) *Differing childhood play experiences of young adults compared to earlier play cohorts have implications for physical, social and academic development*. Poster presentation at the annual meeting of the Association for Psychological Science, Chicago.

Bodrova, E. and Leong, D.J. (1996) 'Scaffolding children's learning in the Zone of Proximal Development', *Primary Voice*, 15: 3–5.

Bruce, T. (2001) *Learning Through Play: Babies, Toddlers and the Foundation Years*. London: Hodder and Stoughton.

Bruner, J.S., Jolly, A. and Sylva, K. (1976). *Play: Its Role in Development and Evolution*. New York: Basic Books.

Canning, N. (2007) 'Children's empowerment in play', *European Early Childhood Education Research Journal*, 15 (2): 227–36.

Central Advisory Council for Education (CACE) (1967) *Children and their Primary Schools* ('The Plowden Report'). London: HMSO.

Craine, W. (2010) 'Is children's play innate?', *Encounter*, 23 (2): 1–3.

Department for Education (2003) *Excellence and Enjoyment: A Strategy for Primary Schools*. Nottingham: DfE.

Diamond, J. and Bond, A.B. (2003) 'A comparative analysis of social play in birds', *Behaviour*, 140 (8/9): 1091–115.

Elkonin, D.B. (2005) 'Theories of play', *Journal of Russian and East European Psychology*, 43 (2): 3–89.

Ensink, K. and Mayes, L.C. (2010) 'The development of mentalisation in children from a theory of mind perspective', *Psychoanalytic Inquiry*, 30: 301–37.

Erikson, E. (1950) *Childhood and Society*. London: Aber.

Freud, S. (1975) [1920] *Beyond the Pleasure Principle*. New York: Norton.

Fromberg, D.P. (2002) *Play and Meaning in Early Childhood Education*. Boston: Allyn & Bacon.

Garner, R. (2007) 'Primary schools "have lost their sense of fun and play"', *Independent, 13 December*.

Gilbert, C. (2006) 2020 *Vision: Report of the Teaching and Learning in 2020 Review Group*. Nottingham: DfES.

Gove (2010) 'Gove's new curriculum: Dangerous Books for Boys', *The Sunday Times*, 12 September. Available at: www.independent.co.uk/news/education-news/primary-school-have-lost-sence-of-fun-and-play-764797.html (accessed July 2011).

Groos, K. (1890) *The Play of Animals*. New York: Appleton.

Hall, S. (1908) *Aspects of Child Life and Education*. Boston, MA: Ginn.

Haydon L. (2008) 'Engaging primary schools learners thought a creative curiculum'. Available at: www.curee-paccts.com/files/publication/1230895566/Engaging_primary_schools_learners_through_a_creative_curriculum.pdf (accessed July 2011).

Isaacs, S. (1929) *The Nursery Years*. London: Routledge and Kegan Paul.

Kravtsov, G.G. and Kravtsova, E.E. (2010) 'Play in L.S. Vygotsky's Nonclassical Psychology', *Journal of Russian and East European Psychology*, 48 (4): 25–41.

Landry, S.H., Smith, K.E. and Swank, P.R. (2009) 'New directions in evaluating social problem solving in childhood: Early precursors and links to adolescent social competence', in C. Lewis and J.I.M. Carpendale (eds), 'Social interaction and the development of executive function', *New Directions in Child and Adolescent Development*, 123: 51–68.

Liu, Y. (2008) 'Understanding play and literacy development in the young child', *Jackson State University Researcher*, 21 (4): 14–50.

Loveless, A. and Thacker, J. (2005) 'Visual Literacy and ICT: "I'm only looking ..."' in S. Wheeler (ed.), *Transforming Primary ICT*. Exeter: Learning Matters. pp. 114–31.

Mastrangelo, S. (2009) 'Harnessing the power of play', *Teaching Exceptional Children*, 42 (1): 34–44.

Nutbrown, C. and Clough, P. (2009) 'Citizenship and inclusion in the early years: understanding and responding to children's perspectives on "belonging"', *International Journal of Early Years Education*, 17 (3): 191–206.

Oliveira, A.F.S., Rossi, A.O., Silva, L.F.R., Lau, M.C. and Barreto, R.E. (2010) 'Play behaviour in nonhuman animals and the animal welfare issue', *Journal of Ethology*, 110: 949–62.

Ortlieb, E.T. (2010) 'The pursuit of play within the curriculum', *Journal of Instructional Psychology*, 37 (3): 241–46.

Palagi, E., Cordoni, G. and Borgognini Tarli, S.M. (2004) 'Immediate and delayed benefits of play behaviour: new evidence from Chimpanzees', *Ethology*, 27 (5): 1257–70.

Palagi, E., Paoli, T. and Borgognini Tarli, S.M. (2006) 'Short-term benefits of play behaviour and conflict prevention in Pan paniscus', *International Journal of Primatology*, 27 (5): 1257–70.

Pellegrini, A. and Boyd, B. (1993) 'The role of play in young childhood development and education: issues in definition and function', in B. Spodek (ed.), *Handbook of Research on the Education of Young Children*. New York: Macmillan. pp. 105–21.

Pellis, S.M. and Iwaniuk, A.N. (2004) 'Evolving a playful brain: A levels of control approach', *International Journal of Comparative Psychology*, 17: 92–118.

Piaget, J. (1999) *Play, Dreams and Imitation in Childhood*. London: Routledge.

Siraj-Blatchford, I. (2009) 'Conceptualising progression in the pedagogy of play and sustained shared thinking in early childhood education: a Vygotskian perspective', *Educational and Child Psychology*, 26 (2): 77–89.

Spencer, H. (1898) *Recent Discussions in Science, Philosophy and Morals*. New York: Appleton.

Strandell, H. (2000) 'What is the use of Children's Play: preparation or social participation?', in H. Penn (ed.), *Early Childhood Services: theory, policy and practice*. Buckingham: Open University Press. pp. 147–57.

Vygotsky, L. (1933) 'Play and its role in the mental development of the child', Voprosy.

Vygotsky, L.S. (1978) *Mind and Society: The Development of Higher Physiological Processes*. Cambridge, MA: Harvard University Press.

Vygotsky, L. (2004) 'Imagination and creativity in childhood', *Journal of Russian and East European Psychology*, 42 (1): 4–84.

Walsh, G., Sproule, L., McGuinness, C., Trew, K., Rafferty, H. and Sheehy, N. (2006) 'An appropriate curriculum for 4–5-year-old children in Northern Ireland: comparing play-based and formal approaches', *Early Years* 26, (2): 201–21.

Winnicott, D. (1971) *Playing and Reality*. London: Tavistock Publications.

Zhang, J., Fallon, M. and Kim, E.J. (2010) 'The Reggio Emilia curricular approach for enhancing play development of young children', *Curriculum and Teaching Dialogue*, 12 (1–2): 85–99.

CHAPTER 2

PLAY PRINCIPLES FOR PRIMARY OR ELEMENTARY AGED CHILDREN

A new paradigm for play

In this chapter we argue for an approach which builds upon early years practice but offers the older learners levels of challenge to enhance and extend their learning as outlined in Chapter 1, rather than merely offering them the same as the early years. Play for this age group may still have the features you might expect to see in the early years, but it is applied to specific situations and aspects of learning to facilitate progress in learning rather than being applied regardless of the context.

We are advocating a fresh look at play and suggest different types of play for 5–11-year-olds linked to a creative approach to the curriculum, and the need to enthuse learners in new ways and bridge the gap in achievement that has been created for particular groups of learners even at this early stage of their schooling. We are engaging with play as part of the process of knowledge creation making connections between different subject domains. In addition, play for older children will provide opportunities to practise skills initially learnt in perhaps more traditionally structured lessons. In order to do this, we are proposing a new paradigm for primary play that uses six roles that primary school children fulfil through different play-based contexts.

Roles for older learners playing

The roles we propose are:

- *child as autonomous learner*
- *child as creative learner*
- *child as investigator*
- *child as problem solver*
- *child as reflective learner*
- *child as social learner.*

What do these mean for the children and all those working with them in an educational setting? The discussion below introduces each of these roles for children in the primary school. It is concerned with explaining why they are important roles for children to assume. Further chapters explore how these can be developed in educational settings.

Child as autonomous learner

It is argued by early years practitioners that play encourages children to be independent and autonomous learners. Research into the behaviour and motivation of older children shows a relationship with the extent to which children feel they have the opportunities to be autonomous and to make important choices about their learning. If the opportunities exist, then children develop a sense of responsibility, are self-motivated to engage in school-based work and remain focused on their learning (McCombs, 2011). Therefore is it clearly necessary for autonomous learning to be a priority of schools.

In order to be independent and autonomous learners children have to develop a number of different strategies and skills, ranging from selecting resources, through working co-operatively with others, to reflecting on what they know, what they need to know and how to find things out. Bennett et al. (1997: 121), after observing play situations in reception classes suggested that play experiences do not automatically develop these abilities in children. What play allows children to do is to explore situations independently if the context has been provided by the adults. This means providing children with not only time and space but also the necessary stimulating resources and initial questions to begin the process of exploring their learning.

Stone and Miyaki (2004: 8) explain how it is 'imperative' that children can self-direct their own learning and they warn that very quickly children can learn to become dependent on their teacher for nearly everything. One extreme example of this was seen by one of the authors when teaching a few years ago. On the third day of the new year, one 10-year-old child put her hand up during a literacy lesson and stated, 'I have reached the end of my page, what should I do now?' In the same class, the children were excited that they were going to have hands-on experience of undertaking science experiments, rather than the teacher demonstrating them. These two examples tell you something of the nature of their previous teacher.

Lack of children's autonomy has been seen in many education systems around the world and to address this, there is a growing body of researchers who suggest that autonomy-promoting education becomes a compulsory element of education (Schinkel, 2010). We do not want children to feel they need to ask questions of their teacher such as the one in the previous paragraph, yet in order to stop children asking we need to create situations where they feel confident about their control over their own learning and how far they can go without checking with the adults. This can be hard for teachers to accept as 'control' of how children are behaving and what they are learning is central to teachers' accountability (see the case study from Croftlands Primary School and how the teachers approached this in Chapter 5). Teachers can feel insecure about what children might be learning if they are given more control over their own learning. It is not always the 'what' that is most important in relation to motivating learners but 'how' the children might learn that can be the change in the locus of control. It is also bounded by the context of schools and the expectations of both teachers' and children's roles.

Simon (1957), writing about organisations, questioned the assumptions behind the rational decision-making process in which individuals clearly define the problem, then generate and evaluate all alternative solutions. From this process, he argued, they then select the best approach before implementing it. He pointed out that people decide rationally only in a limited number of situations. They make choices according to their interpretation of the situation which is often a simplification of a complex one. Rationality is 'bounded'; individuals seldom have access to all relevant information and must rely on a 'strategy of satisfying', that is making the best decision on limited information. Although Simon was writing about organisations and managers' roles within them, his work has resonance when we are exploring the choices available to both teachers and children.

We do know that children learn best when they are motivated and part of that motivation comes from being in more control of their learning and following areas of enquiry in which they are interested. This links to the recent focus in England on 'personalised learning' which aims partly to bridge the gap in achievement between specific groups of learners. We would argue that there is scope for older children to explore areas of interest within the curriculum. This does not mean a return to 'topic work' which used to go on in schools where children created topic books mainly by recreating drawings from factual books and copying large chunks of text in a book specially decorated for the purpose.

The development of research skills (explored in more detail under *Child as investigator*), which might include using technological devices, is of key importance when giving independence and autonomy to learners. This is also important when offering children choices about how they share their research with others and giving them opportunities to communicate their ideas to peers. Teachers should monitor the learning that has taken place and correct any misconceptions or errors.

The following are some examples of how the autonomous child might be seen in the classroom; these and other aspects will be expanded in later chapters through case studies:

- children choosing how to present their work from play-based activities
- children choosing who to work with on play activities
- children choosing the resources including technology that they make use of in their play
- children choosing the location of their play activities.

Child as creative learner

Creativity is a notion that is difficult to define. A more helpful categorisation of the different aspects of creativity comes from Tina Bruce (2004) in her description of layers of creativity:

1   original and world-shaking creativity
2   recreating an idea in a different time and place
3   specialists who create ideas which are important in their field, who may not be famous, but who contribute in important ways
4   everyday creativity that makes life worth living.

It is possible for children to be creative in all areas of the curriculum if we do not see creativity as just the province of the unique and truly original. How a child makes connections between facts, knowledge and skills within subjects taught can show evidence of creativity focusing on Bruce's fourth layer.

Creativity has come to be seen as an essential element of children's education if they are going to be effective adults in the constantly changing future. In the last decade, there has been a focus on creativity in education with the introduction of Creative Partnerships in 2002 (Creative Partnerships, 2010), the National Advisory Committee on Creative and Cultural Education (NACCCE, 1999) and Excellence and Enjoyment (DfE, 2003). What is clear from all these groups is that creativity runs across all areas of the curriculum and is not limited to the more traditional 'creative arts', though in these areas teachers find it easier to make the connections between approaches and the subject matter than in mathematics and science. There is some agreement that a creative learner is one who undertakes 'imaginative activity' (NACCCE, 1999) and learns in innovative, experimental and inventive ways (Jeffrey, 2005).

Craft (2003) raises issues about the language we use to describe creativity and creative activities in particular contexts, identifying how important this issue is as we slip between the use of terms associated with this area and the effects this can have on the values of practice. 'Valuing creative learning, for example, is distinct from valuing creative teaching' (Craft et al., 2007: 4). Our focus here is on the child as a creative learner rather than on creative teaching approaches. We can see creativity as one vehicle to allow 3–8-year-old children to undertake 'possibility thinking' (a key aspect of creative learners). Craft et al., provided opportunities for children:

> to play over extended periods, allowing ideas to develop and combine. Children travelled far in their play, highly motivated by their interests and the development of knowledge. They were often highly engaged, very serious in their playfulness, engaging closely with one another, imagining many scenes, encountering and solving diverse problems. Their play reflected what Sylva et al. (1986) describe as high cognitive challenge. (2007: 4)

Another way of viewing creative learners comes from Willings (1980: 25) who identifies three kinds of 'creative thinking':

- *Adaptive thinking* which is related to the learner making links between apparently unconnected areas
- *Elaborative thinking* which is related to the learner researching, refining or adapting the ideas of others
- *Developmental thinking* which is related to the learner enlarging their conception of self and the world around them.

What is crucial about the child as creative learner associated with play when linked to the literature summarised by Dust (1999) is to break down the 'creative process' into stages or phases and this requires space and time to develop ideas. She suggests that at least four such phases are commonly identified:

1 Preparation
2 Incubation
3 Illumination/revelation
4 Verification/re-framing.

This is supported by the work of Csikszentmihalyi (1997) who coined the phrase 'in the flow' to describe the most productive and fulfilling phases of the creative process. He characterises these by intense concentration, absorption, pleasure and lack of awareness of time passing just as children appear when they are fully engaged in play with their focus solely on their activity. This implies space and uninterrupted time available for the learners to become engrossed in their learning.

The following are some examples of how the creative child might be seen in the classroom; these and other aspects will be expanded in later chapters through case studies:

- children choosing how to present their work from play-based activities through different media
- children being given the space to immerse themselves in play activities
- children utilising resources including technology creatively in their play
- children articulating their discoveries from play activities.

Child as investigator

For the last fifty years, constructivists have seen children as mini-scientists, who discover the world about them through an enquiry-driven interaction with it (see, for example, Confrey, 1990; Piaget, 1970). This way of children viewing the world can be seen in the significant body of educational research that places more emphasis on the importance of process-based learning rather than knowledge-based learning (that is, what children can memorise).

This is generally accepted for children in the EYFS, yet we suggest that this can effectively be continued throughout the primary years and beyond. For example, Futurelab researched and designed a new approach to the curriculum that explored how teachers can support Key Stage 3 children to act as researchers and knowledge creators. The aim of the research was to provide evidence of how 'genuine student participation can be made a reality in classrooms, and how that may be used to inform future [government] policies' (Morgan and Williamson, 2007: 1). It identified how the children became 'researchers' at subject level ('scientific research, historical research, literary research and social research') and also at a more general level 'collecting and interpreting information about a topic, which can then take into account students' own interests, regardless of whether they fit neatly into a subject category or not' (Williamson, 2006).

'A Young Researcher Programme' at the University of Warwick has brought groups of primary aged children, mainly from 9–11 years old, into the university setting to introduce them to research skills around specific areas of interest for their schools. The programme aims to give the children a taste of the academic side of university life by learning what it takes to put together a research project. Some groups have particularly targeted schools in areas where few children aspire to attend university aiming to bridge the gap for these groups. The research has so far focused on play where the children looked at the differences in play from an historical perspective, comparing games and play equipment between now and the past and play between children of different ages and genders, and planning playgrounds to ensure effective and purposeful play. A recent group have started work on learning spaces associated with new builds for their schools. The children are investigators within their own schools working with the staff and other children and often presenting their findings to whole school communities, governing bodies, counsellors and planners who are keen to find out what the children have discovered.

Children learn to use a multitude of skills when investigating such as observing, classifying, communicating, measuring, predicting and inferring (Lee and Yoon, 2008). When using these skills, children interpret the information gained from the world and construct new ideas and understanding. Hansen (2011) and Shepardson (2002) explain how children often draw incorrect conclusions from their observations without the support of adults to help them with their thinking.

The following are some examples of how the investigating child might be seen in the classroom; these and other aspects will be expanded in later chapters through case studies:

- children choosing to investigate aspects of learning
- children presenting their investigations to different audiences
- children using a range of resources including technology for their investigations
- children investigating in different locations.

Child as problem solver

Children are intuitively problem solvers. This is an in-built response to our very human nature. Humans look to solve problems and problem solving is an agreed component of play. Olson cites a parent explaining how video games allow his child to solve problems with his friends. He states, 'it's all about how do you go from this place to that place, or collect the certain things that you need, and combine them in ways that are going to help you to succeed' (2010: 182).

Through play, children are able to develop their understanding of risk. Children use their appraisal of risk to inform their behaviour while playing, for example on playground equipment. Although children do actively seek out activities that offer challenge and excitement, Little and Wyver (2010) identified that 4- and 5-year-olds showed caution in engaging in activities that they felt were beyond their capabilities.

Wyver and Spence (1999) carried out research to challenge a common assumption that play influences problem solving. Their research revealed that there is in fact a reciprocal relationship where problem-solving skills facilitate the development of play skills and vice versa. Furthermore, Ortlieb is emphatic about play (as discovery learning) as 'one of the single greatest ways in which students develop critical thinking skills to solve academic problems in every subject area' (2010: 241).

In addition to the more 'academic' problem solving in relation to science, mathematics and design, play has also been shown to help children to develop resilience to trauma, stress and crisis (Berger and Lahad, 2010). Other research reports how middle-school children use play to help them relax or to work out anger (Olson, 2010). Too specialised for discussion in this book is the role of the play therapist, who often supports children who may be described as oppo-sitional and aggressive (Foulkrod and Davenport, 2010). However, it is worth noting the status that play therapy approaches have within clinical work. For adolescents Spence et al. (2003) used a problem-solving programme to prevent the onset of depression within this age group in a study in Australia, again highlighting the general applicability of problem-solving skills to children as learners at all stages in their lives.

The following are some examples of how the problem-solving child might be seen in the classroom; these and other aspects will be expanded in later chap-ters through case studies:

- children choosing problems to work on
- children deciding how to work on their chosen problems including planning, possibly in collaboration with others
- children demonstrating resilience and perseverance in their problem solving
- children deciding on a potential range of solutions and recommendations.

Child as reflective learner

Teachers and student teachers alike will be very familiar with the term 'reflective learner'. Schön explains that by taking time to deliberately reflect through 'reflec-tion on reflection in action,' a teacher further develops his/her 'repertoire of knowl-edge and experience' through a 'conversation with the situation' (1983: 166).

Psychology literature also points at children developing reflection later in the primary school, with children being able to undertake epistemological thought (that is, 'reflection on the nature of knowledge and the relation between knowledge and reality' (Pillow, 2008: 299)) by age 9–10.

Goodchild (2001) identifies a significant amount of literature that uses the phrase 'blind activity' (in contrast to reflective activity) when referring to children carrying out tasks set by their teacher. He cites Christiansen and Walther who explain, 'blind activity on a task does not ensure learning as intended' (1986: 250).

Allowing children space within the crowded day to enable reflection on learning to take place is vital and has become lost in the focus on the pace of lessons with rapid responses and in many classrooms always having visuals images on the whiteboard to look at during the lessons. This could be facili-tated by reflection on an area learnt that children are encouraged to recreate within their classroom, for example a rain forest, a castle, a Victorian school-room, or more simply by allowing time to collect thoughts before responding, working on visual imagery instead of always being presented with a pre-existing image of characters from books, shapes, locations or anything else which is part of the subject being taught.

The issue of space and time throughout the day for reflection is crucial. It is also important not to make this something which must occur after every lesson or activity so that it becomes routine and in many ways unimportant. Reflection should become part of a range of skills which children can choose to use when it is most appropriate in their learning. It is also not necessarily an activity to be carried out in isolation from other skills and is only of use if there is something learnt from the process that feeds forward into future learning whether positive or negative.

In some of the new designs for schools and learning spaces a different vocabulary is being used (Nair et al., 2005) including 'cave spaces', which are places for individual study, reflection, quiet reading and creative flow, and 'watering holes', which allow learners to gather together for discussion and group work encouraging collaborative learning. Clearly there need to be locations where children can either reflect on their own in a quiet space or can reflect upon learning in a small group discussion.

The following are some examples of how the reflective child might be seen in the classroom; these and other aspects will be expanded in later chapters through case studies:

- space for the opportunity to reflect established as part of the practice in the classroom
- children being allowed to sit and spend time reflecting on their own
- children discussing in small groups their reflections of activities and their learning
- children carrying forward actions/ideas/thoughts from reflections into subsequent activities.

Child as a social learner

It has been widely accepted for some time now that children are social learners (for example, Rogoff, 1998; Vygotsky, 1998; Wood et al., 1978). Collaboration between children can help them to develop their knowledge, language and social skills. Additionally, children find collaboration a valuable learning strategy, and the children explain how collaboration can work effectively when there are good peer relationships (Tunnard and Sharp, 2009).

The awareness and status of relationships in social (and emotional) aspects of learning has been raised since the introduction of the Social and Emotional Aspects of Learning (SEAL) materials into schools in 2005. The five strands within the materials were self-awareness, managing feelings, motivation, empathy and social skills. Research of similar programmes abroad (for example, Maxwell et al., 2008) shows that these types of programmes can be effective in enhancing the well-being of children. Additionally, Hallam's (2009) evaluation of the SEAL pilot indicated that head teachers' feelings about SEAL reiterate this and that head teachers also saw children's engendered positive attitudes towards school. Furthermore, children reported being more supportive of each other which led to stronger relationships.

Given this development in approach to social interaction, we still have numerous situations when children across the 5–11 age range work independently without the benefits of working collaboratively with others (Mercer et al., 2004). However, there is a growing body of research and resources that explore social learning in educational contexts. For example, Wegerif et al. (2004) and Alexander (2009) have focused on learning the skills of dialogue when working with others in the classroom emphasising the social aspects of learning. One key aspect of their work is about 'exploratory talk' which is:

> discussion in which partners engage critically but constructively with each other's ideas. Relevant information is offered for joint consideration. Proposals may be challenged and counter-challenged, but if so reasons are given and alternatives are offered. Agreement is sought as a basis for joint progress. Knowledge is made publicly accountable and reasoning is visible in the talk. (Mercer, 2000: 98)

Additionally, in an exploratory analysis of how a pair of 8-year-old children worked together on mathematical problems, Dekker et al. (2006) identified how the children were not only able to collaboratively solve the problems, but also took an active role in steering their own collaboration.

Bruner (2006) identified how the principle use of play is to socialise children into society and its ways. Seeing children in this light harnesses the innate 'powerful, insightful, valid and valuable' views that children have about issues which are related to them and their lives (MacNaughton, 2007: 460) and play can be seen as 'political work' where it may be necessary for adults to broaden their 'conceptualisations of the relations between children's activities and political activism' (Bosco, 2010: 382). Therefore play as a means to develop children who are social learners is a powerful tool to use in the classroom.

Older children are also motivated to play because of the social element. Research carried out by Olson demonstrated that middle-school children were strongly drawn to the social element of being involved in video games. They liked the excuse to spend time together, and to have something to discuss. Additionally multi-player games can:

> provide a safe space for young people to negotiate rules and discover the boundaries of acceptable behaviour – such as the point where creative strategies are viewed as crossing the line into cheating or taking unfair advantage ... younger children can practice social give-and-take through activities such as collecting and trading game items. (2010: 182)

A key part of being a social learner is the communication between those playing, whether that is adult to child or child to child. Being able to work and communicate with others are lifelong skills and we would want all the children to have achieved a high level of competence in these skills by the time they leave school. Play situations allow children to try out their ideas in a safe and secure environment while learning the rules of a range of different forms of communication including talk, body language and turn taking. Again from the work of Mercer and colleagues come the ground rules for talk which could equally be applied to play for learning as well as more formal learning situations:

> We share our ideas and listen to one another.
>
> We talk one at a time.
>
> We respect each other's opinions.
>
> We give reasons to explain our ideas.
>
> If we disagree we try to ask 'why?'
>
> We always try to agree at the end. (2008: 17)

The following are some examples of how the social child might be seen in the classroom; these and other aspects will be expanded in later chapters through case studies:

- children choosing who to work with on play activities
- children challenging themselves to work outside their friendship groups acknowledging what others might bring to an activity
- children discussing their activities with others and dealing with disagreements
- children collaborating to present their ideas to a wider audience.

New roles for teachers

Alongside the new roles for children as learners, using play requires that teachers and other adults engage in new roles also. These will be discussed in more detail in Chapter 5 but it is worth mentioning here the need for adult involvement to guide, challenge and extend the play of children regardless of age. The adult must also provide the stimulus in relation to the resources, space and time, and create an appropriate atmosphere for collaborative play to take place in an environment of trust and mutual respect.

 Points for reflection

At this stage we ask you to consider your own current practice and review of the child roles which are possible in your classroom or school. Of the roles outlined here which do you think children are able to engage in, when and where? Can you complete Table 2.1?

Table 2.1 Review of the use of child learner roles

Child learner roles	Used often	Used sometimes	Used rarely	Never	Opportunities	Barriers to use
autonomous						
creative						
investigator						
problem solver						
reflective						
social						

 Summary

In this chapter we have introduced a new paradigm for play for older children focusing on the key roles of the learner:

- *child as autonomous learner*
- *child as creative learner*
- *child as investigator*
- *child as problem solver*
- *child as reflective learner*
- *child as a social learner.*

Reflect upon your own practice by thinking about the following questions in relation to play activities:

1 Has your perspective on play and learning changed after reading this chapter?
2 What are your views of the key roles of the learner? Is there anything you would wish to add to the list or take away? Consider why?
3 What do you think children's views would be to considering their learning in this way?

Further reading

Bennett, N., Woods, L. and Rogers, S. (1997) *Teaching Through Play: Teachers' Thinking and Classroom Practice*. Buckingham: Open University Press.

Bruner, J.S. (2006) 'Play as a mode of construing the real', in *In Search of Pedagogy Volume II: The Selected Works of Jerome Bruner*. Abingdon, Osan: Routledge. pp. 57–64.

Stone, S.J. and Miyaki, Y. (2004) *Creating the Multiage Classroom*. Tucson, AZ: Good Year Books.

Wegerif, R., Mercer, N., Littleton, K., Rowe, D. and Dawes, L. (2004) 'Widening Access to Educational Opportunities through teaching Children How to Reason Together'. *Final Report to the Esmée Fairbairn Foundation*.

References

Alexander, R. (ed.) (2009) *Children, their World, their Education: Final Report and Recommendation of the Cambridge Primary Review*. London: Routledge.

Bennett, N., Woods, L. and Rogers, S. (1997) *Teaching Through Play: Teachers' Thinking and Classroom Practice*. Buckingham: Open University Press.

Berger, R. and Lahad, M. (2010) 'A Safe Place: Ways in which nature, play and creativity can help children cope with stress and crisis – establishing the kindergarten as a safe haven where children can develop resiliency', *Early Child Development and Care*, 180 (7): 889–900.

Bosco, F.J. (2010) 'Play, work or activism? Broadening the connections between political and children's geographies', *Children's Geographies*, 8 (4): 381–90.

Bruce, T. (2004) *Cultivating Creativity in Babies, Toddlers and Young Children*, London: Hodder Arnold.

Bruner, J.S. (2006) 'Play as a mode of construing the real', in *In Search of Pedagogy Volume II: The Selected Works of Jerome Bruner*. pp. 57–64.

Christiansen, B. and Walther, G. (1986) 'Task and activity', in B. Christiansen, A.G. Howson and M. Otte (eds), *Perspectives on Mathematics Education*. Dordrecht, Netherlands: D. Reidel. pp. 243–307.

Craft, A. (2003) 'The Limits to Creativity in Education: Dilemmas for the Educator', *British Journal of Educational Studies*, 51 (2): 115–27.

Craft, A., Cremin, T., Burnard, P. and Chappell, K. (2007) 'Developing creative learning through possibility thinking with children aged 3–7', in A. Craft, T. Cremin and P. Burnard (eds), *Creative Learning 3–11 and How We Document It*. London: Trentham. pp. 65–74.

Creative Partnerships (2010) 'Creative partnerships'. Available at: www.creative-partnerships.com/ (accessed July 2011).

Confrey, J. (1990) 'What constructivism implies for teaching', in R.B. Davis, C.A. Maher and N. Noddings (eds), *Constructivist Views on the Teaching and Learning of Mathematics*. Reston, VA: National Council of Teachers of Mathematics (NCTM). pp. 107–22.

Csikszentmihalyi, M. (1997) *Creativity, Flow and the Psychology of Discovery and Invention*. London: Rider.

Dekker, R., Elshout-Mohr, M. and Wood, T. (2006) 'How children regulate their own collaborative learning', *Educational Studies in Mathematics*, 62: 57–79.

Department for Education (2003) *Excellence and Enjoyment: A Strategy for Primary Schools*. Nottingham: DfE.

Dust, K. (1999) *Motive, Means and Opportunity: Creativity Research Review*. London: NESTA.

Foulkrod, K. and Davenport, B.R. (2010) 'An examination of empirically informed practice within case reports of play therapy with aggressive and oppositional children', *International Journal of Play Therapy*, 19 (3): 144–58.

Goodchild, S. (2001) *Students' Goals: A Case Study of Activity in a Mathematics Classroom*. England: Hobbs the Printers.

Hallam, S. (2009) 'An evaluation of the social and emotional aspects of learning (SEAL) programme: promoting positive behaviour, effective learning and well-being in primary school children', *Oxford Review of Education,* 35 (3): 313–30.

Hansen, A. (ed.) (2011) *Children's Errors in Mathematics: Understanding Common Misconceptions in Primary Schools,* 2nd edn. Exeter: Learning Matters Ltd.

Jeffrey, B. (2005) Final Report of the Creative Learning and Student Perspectives Research Project (CLASP), A European Commission Funded project through the Socrates Programme, Action 6.1, Number 2002 – 4682 / 002 – 001. SO2 – 61OBGE. Available at: http://clasp.open.ac.uk/downloads/CLASP_Final_Report. pdf (accessed July 2011).

Lee, J. and Yoon, J.Y. (2008) 'Teaching early childhood teacher candidates how to assess children's inquiry skills in science learning', *Contemporary Issues in Early Childhood,* 9 (3): 265–69.

Little, H. and Wyver, S. (2010) 'Individual differences in children's risk perception and appraisals in outdoor play environments'. *International Journal of Early Years Education,* 18 (4): 297–313.

MacNaughton, G. (2007) 'Young children's rights and public policy: Practices and possibilities for citizenship in the early years', *Children and Society,* 21: 458–69.

Maxwell, C., Aggleton, P., Warwick, I., Yankah, E., Hill, V. and Mehmedbegivic, D. (2008) 'Supporting children's emotional wellbeing and mental health in England: a review', *Health Education,* 108 (4): 272–86.

McCombs, B. (2011) 'Developing responsible and autonomous learners: A key to motivating students'. American Psychological Association. Available at: www.apa. org/education/k12/learners.aspx (accessed July 2011).

Mercer, N. (2000) *Words and Minds: How we use Language to Think Together.* London: Routledge.

Mercer, N. (2008) 'The seeds of time: why classroom dialogue needs a temporal analysis', *Journal of the Learning Sciences,* 17 (1): 33–59.

Mercer, N., Dawes, L., Wegerif, R. and Sams, C. (2004) 'Reasoning as a scientist: ways of helping children to use language to learn science', *British Educational Research Journal,* 30 (3): 359–77.

Morgan, J. and Williamson, B. (2007) *Enquiring minds: Project update January 2007.* Futurelab. Available at: www.enquiringminds.org.uk/pdfs/Enquiring_ Minds_update_0107.pdf (accessed July 2011).

Nair, P., Randall, F. and Lackney, J. (2005) *The Language of School Design: Design Patterns for 21st Century Schools.* South Minneapolis, MN: Design Share.

National Advisory Committee on Creative and Cultural Education (1999) *All Our Futures: Creativity, Culture and Education.* Available at: www.cypni.org.uk/ downloads/alloutfutures.pdf (accessed July 2011).

Olson, C.K. (2010) 'Children's motivations for video game play in the context of normal development', *Review of General Psychology,* 14 (2): 180–87.

Ortlieb, E.T. (2010) 'The pursuit of play within the curriculum', *Journal of Instructional Psychology,* 37 (3): 241–46.

Piaget, J. (1970) *The Science of Education and the Psychology of the Child.* New York, Orion Press.

Pillow, B.H. (2008) 'Development of children's understanding of cognitive activities', *The Journal of Genetic Psychology*, 169 (4): 297–321.

Rogoff, B. (1998) 'Cognition as a collaborative process', in D. Kuhn and R. Siegler (eds), *Cognition, Perception, and Language*, Vol. 2. New York: Wiley. pp. 279–744.

Schinkel, A. (2010) 'Compulsory autonomy-promoting education', *Educational Theory*, 60 (1): 97–116.

Schön, D.A. (1983) *The Reflective Practitioner: How Professionals Think in Action*. New York: Basic Books.

Shepardson, D.P. (2002) 'Bugs, butterflies, and spiders: children's understandings about insects', *International Journal of Science Education*, 24 (6): 627–43.

Simon, H. (1957) 'A Behavioural Model of Rational Choice', in *Models of Man, Social and Rational: Mathematical Essays on Rational Human Behaviour in a Social Setting*. New York: Wiley.

Spence, S.H., Sheffield, J.K., and Donovan, C.L. (2003) 'Preventing adolescent depression: an evaluation of the problem solving for life program', *Journal of Consulting and Clinical Psychology*, 71 (1): 3–13.

Stone, S.J. and Miyaki, Y. (2004) *Creating the Multiage Classroom*. Tucson, AZ: Good Year Books.

Sylva, K., Roy, C. and Painter, M. (1986) *Childwatching at Playgroup and Nursery School*. Oxford: Blackwell.

Tunnard, S. and Sharp, J. (2009) 'Children's views of collaborative learning', *Education 3–13*, 37 (2): 159–64.

Vygotsky, L. (1998) *The Collected Works of L.S. Vygotsky: Volume 5: Child Psychology*. New York: Plenum.

Wegerif, R., Mercer, N., Littleton, K., Rowe, D. and Dawes, L. (2004) 'Widening Access to Educational Opportunities through teaching Children How to Reason Together'. *Final report to the Esmée Fairbairn Foundation*.

Williamson, B. (2006) 'Young people as researchers on Enquiring Minds'. Futurelab. Available at: www.enquiringminds.org.uk/pdfs/Enquiring_Minds_young_researchers. pdf (accessed July 2011).

Willings, D. (1980) *The Creatively Gifted: Recognising and Developing the Creative Personality*. Cambridge: Woodhead Faulkner.

Wood, D., Wood, H. and Middleton, D. (1978) 'An experimental evaluation of four face-to-face teaching strategies', *International Journal of Behavioural Development*, 2: 131–47.

Wyver, S.R. and Spence, S.H. (1999) 'Play and divergent problem solving: evidence supporting a reciprocal relationship', *Early Education and Development*, 10 (4): 419–44.

CHAPTER 3

TYPES OF PLAY FOR PRIMARY SCHOOL CHILDREN

Introduction

In Chapter 2 we put the case for exploring the use of play as a medium for learning across the primary school. In this chapter we develop different types of play suitable for those children. These take the principles of play through an evolving context where there is an increase in the number of subject areas and the range of knowledge expected as children move through their primary education. In each of the different types of play we offer short ideas based upon actual practice or suggested practice to illustrate the possibilities of working in this way and identify some of the skills that children are developing during these activities. Just as the principles of play overlap, so too do the types of play. In Chapter 4 we illustrate the types of play through case studies.

Discriminating between play in school and play in leisure time

 Activity

Sort the statements below (from Pitri) according to whether or not you consider each statement to reflect leisure time only, play in school only, or both.

- Play is any activity that serves a recreational function.
- Pleasure and recreation are necessary but not defining characteristics of play.
- Play is spontaneous and voluntary.
- Play is not obligatory but is freely chosen by the player.
- Play has no extrinsic goals; its motivations are intrinsic.
- Fun itself is intrinsic, and the yield is confined to the player.
- Anyone or anything that intervenes between the player and the play interrupts the fun and distorts his or her performance.
- The validity of the play performance lies in the total commitment to the personal or group demands and rules of the activity.
- Players are concerned with the process of an activity more than its results.
- Goals are self-imposed, and existing rules can be modified.
- Play occurs with familiar objects, or it follows the exploration of unfamiliar objects.
- Children supply their own meanings to activities and control the situations themselves.
- In classroom environments, teachers tend to emphasize the 'seriousness' in play.
- Educational play is, indeed, serious in that the player is deeply absorbed in enjoyment.
- The role of the adult in children's play is not that of an instructor or entertainer, but rather of a friend. (2001: 47)

Would you add any more statements? Are there any you would disagree with? Talk with a colleague about where you placed the statements, and discuss the extent to which you both agree about the placement.

According to Bishop and Curtis:

> Children have a play repertoire which they dip into according to the circumstances in which they find themselves, varying their games according to the weather, the physical surroundings, the number of playmates and the length of time available. (2001: 10–11)

The types of play we present in this chapter can be observed during the leisure time of 5–11-year-old children. However, we explore the types of play here in relation to utilising these play types during school time as a teaching strategy. We argue that drawing on how children often choose to behave when they are relaxed and motivated – whether alone or in a social group – enhances children's enjoyment of learning at school and therefore their educational attainment.

Types of play

We suggest the following types of play to enhance learning in the primary school:

- artistic or design play
- controlled imaginary play/social dramatic play
- exploratory play
- games play
- integrated play
- play using the whole school environment and beyond
- replication play
- small world play
- role play
- virtual play.

Each of these is discussed in more detail below and brief ideas for how they might be implemented in school are given. More detailed case studies are presented in Chapter 4.

Artistic play

Artistic play is a term not commonly used in our education system. This may be because our society has tended to focus on the teaching and success of the traditional subjects of English, mathematics and science. However, Bulatova suggests that:

> attempts to accomplish pedagogical tasks only by rational and logical schemas often turn out to be inadequate. Science does not have a full arsenal of expressive means sufficient to explain the phenomena of life in all its fullness, vividness, and variety. (2006: 71)

Typical approaches to learning encourage children to carefully plan and logically systemise the steps they will take to achieve their (or their teacher's) desired outcome. Artistic play is counter to this approach. The key of artistic or design play is the *process* the participant goes through to learn something about themselves or the concept they are exploring.

In other countries artistic play is used as a medium for learning a range of subjects. For example, Anttila (2007: 43) writes about using 'artistic experiences and dance play' in a Finnish elementary school to enhance children's well-being by helping them to be conscious of their thinking. 'The idea of children's empowerment ... remained an undercurrent' (2007: 44). In Japan artistic play is referred to as 'zoukei-asobi' (Fujie, 2003) where the children

- do not have a particular image in mind as they begin
- enjoy the visual and tactile or kinaesthetic experience gained as they are working with the materials
- routinely enjoy zoukei-asobi beyond the classroom, where any space provides inspiration.

Artistic play is also common within theology. For example, Goto reflects on how a teacher used artistic play to support members of a Christian church to reaffirm their identity. Her findings show how artistic play enabled the Japanese–American congregation to resolve tensions and experience 'true selves' (2008: 440). The Alliance for Jewish Renewal also sees the value in artistic play, using play as a vehicle to deeper religious experience (Weissler, 2007). In a process that is not dissimilar to zoukei-asobi, Weissler cites Milgram who writes:

> Rough, untutored shapes responding to a biblical passage, shapes resembling something or nothing – these will be invested with whatever meaning the maker gives them. There is no right or wrong. The idea is to give the hands autonomy, to be a child, to allow the soul to play and to make shapes that the rational mind may at first consider worthless. Once those forms find their voice, they can become powerful personal metaphors resonating [with] the individual's very nature and embodying a deep personal experience of the text. (2007: 361)

 Ideas

Social and emotional aspects of learning (SEAL)

One of the themes of the English SEAL programme is 'Good to be me'. Providing children with a malleable material such as clay can offer them a medium to explore what it is to 'be me'. During the process children can explore their own feelings of self-belief through the media, emerging with a product that they can reflect upon with their peers.

 Curriculum links

SEAL links to PSHE and Citizenship

By undertaking an artistic play approach to SEAL, children are able to explain their views on issues that affect them, recognise their worth as individuals, reflect on spiritual, moral, social and cultural issues using imagination to understand their own and others' experiences, and care about others' feelings.

Controlled imaginary play/social dramatic play

It is widely known that imaginary friends appear during preschool age (Taylor et al. 2004) and as children become older these companions continue to have a place (Cohen and MacKeith, 1991; Pearson et al. 2001; Taylor et al. 2004). It is also possible that there is a correlation between having imaginary friends or enacting imaginary people and possessing a deeper emotional understanding (Taylor et al. 2004).

Controlled imaginary or social dramatic play builds on children's propensity to accept the possibility of stepping into imaginary worlds, playing with imaginary friends and being imaginary characters. This play type emphasises the child as a social learner because it allows opportunities to work with others, to speak to them and to listen to their contributions, perhaps developing their emotional understanding further. Saifer (2010) argues that this type of play (which he calls 'higher order play') leads to higher order thinking in children of all ages.

 Ideas

Using story to prompt controlled imaginary play

Welsch (2008) found that play within a story context enables children to investigate social relationships and interactions, encouraging personal responses as well as enhanced comprehension of the literature. *Learning Languages Through Fairy Tales* (Harty and Cartwright, 2008) is an approach to learning languages based on the familiar fairy stories of Goldilocks and the Three Bears and The Three Billy Goats Gruff. This pack of resources for language teaching offers a range of games to support learning but could also be used to explore the stories in an imaginary play environment though spoken in one of the four languages available in the pack.

Stories could be one trigger for the notion of 'imaginary frames' introduced by Marjanovi-Shane and Beljanski-Ristić where 'a recursive process ... takes place on different but related time scales' (2008: 94). In imaginary frames, children are able to experience a dynamic interplay between the ideas within a context and between each other. El'Koninova (2002) presents a similar model, where children are able to undertake activity that mediates relationships with others and also within the context presented.

Exploratory play

This kind of play puts the child in the role of explorer or investigator and can involve simple activities like playing with magnets or batteries and bulbs and exploring the outcomes of trial and error. In their research study asking middle-school aged children about their preferences for types of play, Kinzie and Joseph (2008) found that in virtual games 'explorative play' could be undertaken when physical space and travel are simulated. By hiding certain areas, children are able to discover new areas and challenges as they are revealed. Schulz and Bonawitz (2007) found that children engage in more exploratory play when the evidence or resources they are provided with are confounded, and that they are able to selectively explore them in order to identify cause and effect.

Ideas

Making stars

A class of 9- and 10-year-olds were studying space and used exploratory play to explore how to draw stars using a compass. They started by learning to draw a 5cm radius circle with a compass. Keeping the compass set on the radius (5cm) they then marked off that length all around the circle. These marks gave them the six points of the star which could then be joined up with a pencil and a ruler to form the star. Having learnt about how to draw one star they were then able to play to form other stars experimenting with the use of a compass, ruler and pencil to create their designs.

Curriculum links

The skills used in this idea could include finer motor skills, use of a ruler and developing knowledge of different star shapes.

Vanslova (2001) writes about the notion of 'museum pedagogy' which uses children as explorers. It shows that exploratory play can not only be used to think about developing understanding from exploring physical resources, but can also encourage children to be introspective. For example, after a visit to an Armory Museum the 7–8-year-old children were asked the question, 'Who is the strongest?' The children came to the 'main idea: muscular strength is very important, of course, but that is not the main strength a person has. The most important strength is the strength of the human spirit' (2001: 82).

Games play

Games with rules have been in existence for thousands of years. Playing games can improve children's cognitive ability, as well as their physical, emotional and behavioural health (see Kinzie and Joseph, 2008) irrespective of their age. It is on this basis that we include games as a key type of play.

Physical games
According to Pellegrini et al. (2004) there are three global categorisations of physical games. These are chase games, ball games and jumping/verbal games. They suggest chase games (for example, tag) are the simplest, involving children taking turns to run after each other. Ball games (for example, football,

dodgeball) tend to have more rules and so they are more complicated. Jumping/verbal games use chants, rhymes or songs and typically include physical activity such as clapping, skipping or hopscotch.

Jarvis concluded that football played by 4–6-year-old children during playtimes created a 'complexity of boys' social development in a synthesis of physical, social and competitive play emerging from the football games' (2007: 256) that the teachers had not realised. These outcomes can be built upon in class-based lessons. For example, Light (2006) identified how games in physical education can encourage the relationships between thinking and moving, skill execution and understanding.

Other games

 Ideas

Games can take many forms from simple pelmanism games, where children have to recognise and remember the positions of objects or symbols on cards which can help to consolidate skills in mathematics, English, science or any other subject in the primary curriculum, to complex simulations. Card games and board games can improve children's skills, knowledge, understanding and appreciation of concepts, as well as build team-work skills. (Ramani and Siegler, 2008; Smith and Munro, 2009)

Computer games can be a significant part of children's leisure time. There are many advocates who state that the use of computer games enhances children's educational experience (for example, Abrams, 2009; Alberti, 2008; and Gee, 2003 all purport digital literacies encourage traditional literacy understanding). However, the results are mixed (Kim and Chang, 2010). Therefore when you are planning to use computer games in your teaching, consider what the desired learning outcome is and the extent to which the game helps children achieve it. Although motivational, the key to effective play is that it enhances learning.

 Ideas

The internet offers a wide range of virtual games to link with subjects in the primary curriculum. Often these are using the computer to complete a task, for example you can play a virtual jousting game at www.show.me.uk/topicpage/teachers/tTudors.html as part of looking at Tudor England and life in castles.

Points for reflection

Valuing game debriefs

Several researchers (for example, Kriz, 2004; Peters and Vissert, 2004) have shown that debriefing after a game is more likely to encourage learning to happen. Think about a time when you have played a game with children. To what extent did you encourage them to think about how they played the game, what steps led to the winner achieving their goal, and what could have been done differently in another game that is the same or related?

Integrated play

Integrated approaches are well recognised in many schools worldwide (Bunnell, 2010; VanTassel-Baska and Wood, 2009). Bennett et al. (1997) describe play as an integrating mechanism providing a context in which children can draw on their past experiences making connections between them, representing their experiences in different ways and exploring and creating meaning. So play is an integrating process which, ideally throughout lifelong learning, becomes just one of the tools or mediums for learning regardless of the age of the learner. In this way we can see play activities integrated into teachers' planning of appropriate activities for all learners. Examples can often be seen in teachers' practice where they are challenged to reconsider the needs of a specific group of learners and how to engage them in the learning process. Harris (2007) suggests that it is not just play-based activity per se that is required for integrated play; is how the environment embodies play qualities as experiences and interactions play out.

 Ideas

Louise Bartlett (2006) shows in a Teachers' TV video her work with a class of 10- and 11-year-olds where she integrates role play into a carousel of activities to support different aspects of writing, which she found particularly helps the boys in the class. Role play is just one speaking and listening activity planned to assist children to structure their written work.

Play using the whole school environment and beyond

A typical classroom design implicitly encourages individual work. Even when arranged in groups, tables are often too large for children to work in a truly collaborative fashion with peers. Indeed, Greenwood et al. (2002) observed that the majority of children's time in the classroom was spent in managing tasks and inappropriate behaviour, instead of engaging academically in their activity. Moving around the school and further afield enables children to work in different settings, often less constrained by the physical layout of the classroom, and enjoy a more playful approach which in turn improves on-task behaviour (Tsao, 2010).

Other indoor areas

Within any school environment there are numerous indoor areas that can be used. Schools may have a hall, information and communication technology (ICT) suites, spare classrooms, corridor areas, space in the staffroom or the school entrance, or withdrawal rooms where it is possible to create a learning environment that is different to the regular classroom space.

 Points for reflection

Think about your school or the last school you visited and reflect on how the space is used. Are there spaces that are used for several different functions, for example a hall for dining and physical activities? Could other spaces be utilised further?

Outdoor play

The school's grounds are a free and easily accessible location that takes children into the outdoors. The EYFS emphasises the importance of the outdoors as a key area for children's learning to take place. Yet it is not just in the early years that children enjoy playing outside. For example, Cherney and London (2005) found that 68 per cent of boys and 50 per cent of girls aged 5–13 years preferred to undertake activities outdoors. Part of this discussion about the use of outdoor environments centres on the debate about the place of physical exercise for children as a crucial part of their health and development. Play undertaken during children's leisure time outdoors has appeared to decrease in the last decade yet outdoor play offers 'tremendous potential' for child development (Staempfli, 2009). When playing outdoors, children's physical activity level increases (Aarts et al. 2010). Physical activity is good for children's general health but it also allows children to explore their physical boundaries, test their physical and mental abilities, use initiative, and take risks and engage with challenges. Furthermore, children's play outside offers them opportunities for physical activity the lack of which continues to be a concern in the light of childhood obesity (Cooper et al. 2010).

Ideas

Often large-scale play takes place in the school playground. For example, marking out the scale of a narrow boat to see exactly how big the living quarters where and then trying to fit children into the space can be carried out in the playground where it is possible to mark out the actual size of the boat, rather than looking at models in the classroom whilst sitting at a table. This can be a good starting point for large-scale activities.

Beyond the school

Larson (2006: 322) talks about how learning outside the school is a 'practice in which the classroom walls are breached and students learn in more complex ways'. She explains how children can use their own and others' practices to learn not just what is expected in school, but what will support their 'capacity to authentically participate in a global information economy'. However, Noel reminds us that 'learning is optimized only when teachers actively integrate the content of the field trip with the curriculum' (2007: 43). Therefore meaningful experiences only occur when there is a flexible integration of curriculum subjects, age-related activities, and appropriate preparation and follow-up. Close liaison with staff at the location will help with planning for this (Coughlin, 2010).

Virtual environments

Although there are obvious benefits to being physically out of the classroom and outdoors, another way to look at exploring the environment outside the classroom is to do so virtually. A growing range of digital resources are available for schools to do this. For example, 'Digimap for schools' (http://digimap-forschools.edina.ac.uk/login.html) is an online resource from Ordinance Survey which provides the most detailed digital mapping of Great Britain. This offers teachers and children opportunities to explore maps at different scales of detail linking to geographical skills associated with map work with children between the ages of 7 and 11.

Replication play

Although this could be seen as a return to the replication play discussed by Groos (1898) and Hall (1908), by revisiting roles and activities associated with our current culture we are proposing a different view of this for older learners. We propose that, instead of looking at this type of play from an anthropological perspective, we can see this as providing opportunities for children to try out roles in society and experience activities from the perspective of different cultures. The key to replication play is that the children are undertaking *authentic* tasks while they are enacting a particular role.

An example of replication play is children enacting the role of a scientist. The *MyScience* initiative in Australia (www.myscience.com.au) uses this approach. Teachers, children and volunteer mentor scientists work collaboratively as learners to conduct authentic scientific investigations to explore their own questions.

 Ideas

Although you may not have access to mentor scientists in your school, it could be possible to instigate this type of approach using ICT to communicate between children, children and teachers, children and experts (for example, mathematicians or scientists), and teachers and experts. This has become an educational feature of web-based environments (Way and Beardon, 2003).

Another example of replication play would be to take the part of a person in history to explore their activities, not so they could be mimicked exactly but to allow empathy and understanding of the way people lived in different periods of history.

Small world play

In early childhood education, small-world play (Levy, 2008) utilises miniature equipment that represents objects that are familiar to children, for example a farmyard with animals, a house with furniture and a family, or a railway track with a station. Although there is no research related to small world play beyond the EYFS, our own anecdotal evidence tells us that children in primary schools continue to create and engage with small world play, including fantasy play. For some, fantasy play continues into adulthood with re-enactments of war-time battles or games such as 'Dungeons and Dragons'.

 Ideas

The creation of small world play environments can encourage speaking and listening and creative writing activities. Large trays that are commonly used in early years settings – the kind that are used on building sites for mixing on which are readily available – can be ideal for older children to create patterns or small worlds using a variety of resources. Small world play can link to play outside the classroom with scale models used to design playground environments including garden areas.

Role play

According to Blatner (1995), in many ways 'role play is nothing more than rehearsal'. He goes on to liken the activity to the practice of skills by musicians, footballers, actors or even fire fighters. We tend to think immediately of actors when we think of roles but people do take on different kinds of roles throughout their lives. The play context allows the participants to explore roles that they may or may not undertake in 'real life'. From drama education literature (for example, Winston and Tandy, 2009; Neelands, 2011; Clipson-Boyles, 2011) taking on a role is not as easy as simply being assigned a role and being able to play it straight away. There need to be opportunities to try on a role with warm ups to establish trust within the group before a full blown role play takes place. This contrasts with the spontaneous role play that can occur with children when the impetus and ideas come from them rather than the stimulus being created by the adults. The interpersonal skills required in role play can be underestimated by those supporting the learning but careful preparation can support all those involved in the activities. Often role play links to the child as a social learner allowing opportunities for speaking and listening across the curriculum. Pretend play helps children develop story telling skills, imagination and grammar for English, English as an additional language (EAL) and modern foreign languages (MFL).

 Ideas

Travel by aeroplane as part of a transport theme

A unit about transport might lead to an area created to allow children to explore ideas and knowledge about travel by air. Walls can be painted to form the shape of the aeroplane windows. A large black sheet can be draped from the ceiling to partition this section of the class from the rest of the classroom activities. Chairs can be arranged in rows as in a plane with seats for the pilot and co-pilot as well as seats for the stewards. A trolley placed in the aisle can distribute drinks, food and duty free goods. Trays can be available for meals, as can magazines for reading. Pockets can be made to go over the backs of the chairs in front to hold magazines, safety cards and sick bags which the children can help to make. The initial idea for the area for the role play can come from a teacher, but the children in the class should develop this by adding resources and suggesting additions as their play in this area progresses. Some of the class may have previously travelled by air and could therefore draw upon this experience to play specific roles and to assist others in the class to engage with the context.

Curriculum links

The skills used in this case study could include speaking, listening, understanding of the context of travel by air and others depending upon the level of engagement and participation.

Virtual play

Virtual play continues to grow in popularity as a pastime and as games and the internet become more reliable, faster and cheaper, technology is creating significant changes to cultural and social behaviours (Marsh, 2010). Some educational researchers (Davies, 2009; Thomas, 2007) suggest that teachers should not make a distinction between virtual and real experiences by trying to separate them because play happens on a continuum that contains both online and offline experiences. Marsh defines virtual play as:

> an activity which is complex, multi-faceted and context-dependent ... [in] immersive 2D or 3D simulations of persistent space in which users adopt an avatar in order to represent themselves and interact with others. They may or may not include game elements. (2010: 24)

Noss and Hoyles (1996: 59) propose that computers can open 'windows on mathematical meaning' in a way that other tools or games cannot. They explain that for a tool to enter into a relationship with its user, it must 'afford the user expressive power: the user must be capable of expressing thoughts and feelings with it. It is not enough for the tool to merely "be there", it must enter into the user's thoughts, actions and language'. This was seen in the EU funded Playground Project (2001) (http://playground.ioe.ac.uk/) that built computer environments for 4–8-year-olds in the UK, Portugal, Slovenia and Sweden to play, design and create games. The project aimed to harness children's playfulness, creative potential and exploratory spirit, allowing them to enter into abstract and formal ways of thinking. The notion of a virtual playground was a place to play *with* rules, rather than to play *by* them. This is more akin to the virtual environment that Noss and Hoyles were referring to.

 Ideas

Logo is a virtual environment that children can programme in order to design their own micro worlds. Copying and pasting pictures of objects onto the screen and setting up a maze for another child to negotiate is one simple way that the children can begin to explore in this micro world.

Table 3.1 Mapping types of play with the play principles

	Play principles					
	Autonomous learner	Creative learner	Investigator	Problem solver	Reflective learner	Social learner
Types of play Artistic or design play						
Controlled imaginary/ social dramatic play						
Exploratory play						
Games play						
Integrated play						
Play using the whole school environment and beyond						
Replication play						
Role play						
Virtual play						

Summary

We have offered a view of different types of play. Some of these you may already use in your school. However, to establish these requires time, space and understanding of the perspectives to be taken. Reflect on the play principles introduced in Chapter 2. Identify the extent to which each principle is present. Completing Table 3.1 may help you. Consider which you already use and which there may be issues with in relation to implementing.

Further reading

Berry, M. (2005) 'A virtual learning environment in primary education'. Available at: www.worldecitizens.net/ftp/Primary%20VLE.pdf (accessed July 2011).

Gee, J. (2003). *What Video Games Have to Teach us About Learning and Literacy*. New York: Macmillan.

References

Aarts, M., Wendel-Vox, W., van Oers, H., van de Goor, I. and Schuit, A.J. (2010) 'Environmental determinants of outdoor play in children: a large-scale cross-sectional study', *American Journal of Preventive Medicine*, 39 (3): 212–19.

Abrams, S.S. (2009) 'A gaming frame of mind: digital contexts and academic implications', *Educational Media International*, 46 (4): 335–47.

Alberti, J. (2008) 'The game of reading and writing: How video games reframe our understanding of literacy', *Computers and Composition*, 25: 258–269.

Anttila, E. (2007) 'Searching for a dialogue in dance education: a teacher's story', *Dance Research Journal*, 39 (2): 42–57.

Bartlett, L. (2006) 'KS2 Literacy – Boys' Writing 2'. Available at: www. schools world. tv/videos/ks2-literacy-boys-writing-2 (accessed July 2011).

Bennett, N., Wood, L. and Rogers, S. (1997) *Teaching Through Play: Teachers' Thinking and Classroom Practise*. Buckingham: Open University Press.

Bishop, J.C. and Curtis, M. (2001) *Play Today in the Primary School Playground: Life, Learning and Creativity*. Buckingham: Open University Press.

Blatner, A. (1995) 'Drama in education as mental hygiene: A child psychiatrist's perspective', *Youth Theatre Journal*, 9: 92–6.

Bulatova, O.S. (2006) 'On the role of the artistic element in pedagogical activity', *Russian Education and Society*, 47 (6): 71–85.

Bunnell, T. (2010) 'The momentum behind the International Primary Curriculum in schools in England', *Journal of Curriculum Studies*, 42 (4): 471–86.

Cherney, I.D. and London, K. (2005) 'Gender-linked differences in the toys, television shows, computer games, and outdoor activities of 5- to 13-year-old children', *Sex Roles*, 54: 717–26.

Clipson-Boyles, S. (2001) *Teaching the Primary Curriculum Through Drama: A Practical Approach*. London: Routledge.

Cohen, D. and MacKeith, S.A. (1991) *The Development of Imagination: The Private Worlds of Childhood*. London: Routledge.

Cooper, A.R., Page, A.S., Wheeler, B.W., Hillsdon, M., Griew, P. and Jago, R. (2010) 'Patterns of GPS measured time outdoors after school and objective physical activity in English children: the PEACH project', *International Journal of Behavioral Nutrition and Physical Activity*, 7 (1): 31.

Coughlin, P.K. (2010) 'Making Field Trips Count: Collaborating for Meaningful Experiences', *Social Studies*, 101: 200–10.

Davies, J. (m ,2009) 'Online connections, collaborations, chronicles and crossings', in R. Willett, M. Robinson and J. Marsh (eds), *Play, Creativity and Digital Cultures*. New York: Routledge.

El'Koninova, L.I. (2002) 'The object orientation of children's play in the context of understanding imaginary space-time in play and in stories', *Journal of Russian and East European Psychology*, 39 (2): 30–51.

Fujie, M. (2003) 'A comparative study of artistic play and zoukei-asobi', *Journal of Aesthetic Education*, 37 (4): 107–14.

Gee, J. (2003). *What Video Games Have to Teach us About Learning and Literacy*. New York: Macmillan.

Goto, C.T. (2008) 'Pretending to be Japanese: artistic play in a Japanese-American church and family', *Religious Education*, 103 (4): 440–55.

Greenwood, C.R., Horton, B.T. and Utley, C.A. (2002) 'Academic engagement: Current perspectives on research and practice', *School Psychology Review*, 31 (3): 328–50.

Groos, K. (1898) *The Play of Animals*. New York: Appleton.

Hall, S. (1908) *Aspects of Child Life and Education*. Boston, MA: Ginn.

Harris, P. (2007) 'Developing an integrated play-based pedagogy in preservice teacher education: A self-study', *Studying Teacher Education*, 3 (2): 135–54.

Harty, L. and Cartwright, S. (2008) *Learning Languages Through Fairy Tales*. London: Optimus Education.

Jarvis, P. (2007) 'Dangerous activities within an invisible playground: a study of emergent male football play and teachers' perspectives of outdoor free play in the early years of primary school', *International Journal of Early Years Education*, 15 (3): 245–59.

Kim, S. and Chang, M. (2010) 'Computer games for the math achievement of diverse students', *Educational Technology and Society*, 13 (3): 224–32.

Kinzie, M.B. and Joseph, D.R.D. (2008) 'Gender differences in game activity preferences of middle school children: implications for educational game design', *Educational Technology Research and Development*, 56: 643–63.

Kriz, W.C. (2004) 'Creating effective learning environments and learning organizations through gaming simulation design', *Simulation & Gaming*, 34 (4): 495–511.

Larson, J. (2006) 'Multiple literacies, curriculum, and instruction in early childhood and elementary school', *Theory Into Practice*, 45 (4): 319–27.

Levy, R. (2008) '"Third spaces" are interesting places: Applying "third space theory" to nursery aged children's constructions of themselves as readers', *Journal of Early Childhood Literacy*, 8 (1): 43–66.

Light, R. (2006) 'Game sense: innovation or just good coaching?', *Journal of Physical Education New Zealand*, 39: 8–19.

Marjanovi-Shane, A. and Beljanski-Ristić, L. (2008) 'From play to art – from experience to insight', *Mind, Culture and Activity*, 15: 93–114.

Marsh, J. (2010) 'Young children's play in online virtual worlds', *Journal of Early Childhood Research*, 8 (1): 23–39.

Neelands, J. (2011) 'Drama as creative learning', in J. Sefton-Green, P. Thomson, K. Jones and L. Bresler (eds), *Routledge International Handbook of Creative Learning*. London: Routledge.

Noel, A.M. (2007) 'Elements of a winning field trip', *Kappa Delta Pi Record*, 44 (1): 42–4.

Noss, R. and Hoyles, C. (1996) *Windows on Mathematical Meanings: Learning Cultures and Computers*. Dordrect: Kluwer Academic Publishers.

Pearson, D., Rouse, H., Doswell, S., Ainsworth, C., Dawson, O., Simms, K., Edwards, L. and Faulconbridge, J. (2001) 'Prevalence of imaginary companions in a normal child population', *Child: Care, Health and Development*, 27: 12–22.

Pellegrini, A.D., Blatchford, P., Kato, K. and Baines, E. (2004) 'A short-term longitudinal study of children's playground games in primary school: implications for adjustment to school and social adjustment in the USA and the UK', *Social Development*, 13 (1): 107–23.

Peters, V. and Vissert, G. (2004) 'A simple classification model for debriefing simulation games', *Simulation & Gaming*, 35 (1): 70–84.

Pitri, E. (2007) 'The role of artistic play in problem solving', *Art Education*, 54 (3): 46–51.

Ramani, G.B. and Siegler, R.S. (2008) 'Promoting broad and stable improvements in low-income children's numerical knowledge through playing number board games', *Child Development,* 79 (2): 375–94.

Saifer, S, (2010) 'Higher order play and its role in development and education', *Psychological Science and Education,* Issue 3: 48–61.

Schulz, L.E and Bonawitz, E. B. (2007) 'Serious fun: preschoolers engage in more exploratory play when evidence is confounded', *Developmental Psychology*, 43 (4): 1045–50.

Smith, D.R. and Munro, E. (2009) 'Educational card games', *Physics Education*, 44: 479–83.

Staempfli, M.B (2009) 'Reintroducing adventure into children's outdoor play environments', *Environment and Behaviour,* 41 (2): 268–80.

Taylor, M., Carlson, S.M., Maring, B.L., Gerow, L and Charley, C.M. (2004) 'The characteristics and correlates of fantasy in school-age children: imaginary companions, impersonation, and social understanding', *Developmental Psychology,* 40 (6): 1173–87.

Thomas, A. (2007) *Youth Online: Identity and Literacy in the Digital Age.* New York: Peter Lang.

The National Centre for Languages: Primary Languages http://www.primary languages.org.uk/resources/cilt_library/events_and_displays.aspx (accessed 30 August 2010).

Tsao, Y-Ling (2010) 'Integrating the design mathematical trail in mathematics curriculum for the sixth grade student', *Journal of Instructional Psychology*, 37 (1): 81–96.

Vanslova, E.G. (2001) 'Museum pedagogy', *Education and Society,* 43 (12): 76–84.

VanTassel-Baska, J. and Wood, S. (2009) 'The integrated curriculum model (ICM)', *Learning and Individual Differences,* 20: 345–57.

Way, J. and Beardon, T. (2003) 'Expanding horizons: the potential of the Internet to enhance learning', in J. Way and T. Beardon (eds), *ICT and Primary Mathematics.* Maidenhead: Open University Press. pp. 91–121.

Welsch, J.G. (2008) 'Playing within and beyond the story: encouraging book-related pretend play', *Reading Teacher,* 62 (2): 138–48.

Weissler, C. (2007) '"Art is spirituality!": practice, play and experiential learning in the jewish renewal movement', *Material Religion,* 3 (3): 354–79.

Winston, J. and Tandy, M. (2009) *Beginning Drama 4–11*, 3rd edn. London: David Fulton.

CHAPTER 4

PLAY IN THE PRIMARY CURRICULUM

Introduction

In the previous chapters we provided a theoretical framework for the remainder of the book. Chapter 1 discussed a range of definitions of play and highlighted the need for you to develop your own definition of 'play'. Chapter 2 identified the principles that underpin the notion of play in this book. It presented children as autonomous, creative, investigating, problem-solving, reflective and social learners. This shifts the way some may conceptualise teaching. Rather than the teacher being the 'expert' who is required to fill children's knowledge stores as if they are empty vessels, these principles identify all children as having the potential to learn complex concepts at any age. Finally, Chapter 3 presented types of play that can be used in the primary school by teachers in the context of the principles that underpin the notion of play.

The purpose of this chapter is to illustrate through case studies how different types of play have been utilised by teachers and trainee teachers to create playful learning experiences for a range of primary aged children.

Overview of case studies

The case studies below demonstrate a range of ways that teachers and children have used play-based approaches to learning. As each case study is presented, curriculum links are provided and an explanation of the type of play and the play principles that are evident is also given. These examples are by no means exhaustive. We hope that they will act as a catalyst for you to try play-based approaches in your teaching as well as illustrate the principles and types of play outlined in earlier chapters.

Artistic play

Artistic play is arguably one of the most difficult types of play to set up and develop with children if it is followed to the letter. Although the case study below begins in a structured way (not often associated with artistic play), the children developed their own products as a result of a freeing of the constraints after the initial teacher input. More authentic artistic play can be seen as the activity develops over time, particularly in relation to children having deep emotional responses to their products.

 Case study: Random art

This case study presents one type of artistic play where the children were exploring random numbers. The teacher, a mathematics co-ordinator, explains ...

'I was getting frustrated because the word "random" had slipped into the way that they were speaking to each other all the time at school. They would say things in response to my questions like, "Well, this is probably really random but ..." or when another pupil came into the class they might comment about the child's "random" query. It was driving me crazy because I didn't like the casual way they were speaking and I thought, from a maths perspective, that it would be a good chance to explore randomness with them.

'First, we talked about what random meant and related it to rolling a dice and tossing a coin and drawing lottery numbers. Then I explained that we were going to explore randomness through art. They liked that idea. I modelled it first and then they used the laptops. In pairs they created lines that were 1, 2, 3, 4, 5 and 6 units wide. They made a stock of those. Then they rolled a die and whatever number came up they put a line of that width. Then they rolled again and that was the gap. Then they kept repeating that pattern so it ended up looking like a bar code. This (see Figure 4.1) is one example.

'All of this really captured their imaginations. They wanted to produce more so we talked about other ways that they could generate random numbers. Some children also suggested using colour and that brought in other curriculum areas like design and we talked about not having too many. In this piece (see Figure 4.2) the children threw two dice to identify the length of the sides of the rectangles and then they spun a spinner to identify the colour of the rectangles. In this example (see Figure 4.3) the children created six circles of different sizes and a dice identified the circle they were going to use. They created a spinner with north, south, east and west on it and this dictated what direction the next circle was translated in. If there was no space they kept going until there was. They made up the rule that they had to touch. Sometimes they couldn't place one they created. Then they drew blocks out of a bag to identify the colour to use.

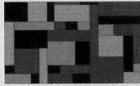

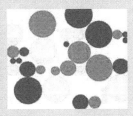

Figure 4.1 Sample 1   **Figure 4.2** Sample 2   **Figure 4.3** Sample 3

'What I found really interesting from this work is that the children did begin to appreciate what randomness as a concept was. And they found it hard! Some groups created art that wasn't particularly aesthetically pleasing which challenged them and some struggled to let the random generator do its work because they had an opinion on what looked right. The good thing about using the computers to generate the work is that they could do it quickly and it looked clean. They would start another one based on what they had learnt from the previous iteration. I couldn't stop them doing it! They did it at home and they got more and more creative about how to generate random numbers. And what's more, they stopped using "random" in a slang way in the class! That was a result for me too.'

 Curriculum links

The skills used in this idea could include exploring a range of starting points for art, using a range of materials including ICT, investigating materials and processes, selecting and using appropriate mathematical equipment and explaining reasoning.

Controlled imaginary play

In our experience teachers often hold a misconception that older children cannot engage in imaginary play. However, we have found that when given the context older children enter into this type of play very readily and with great motivation. This example of controlled imaginary play is based upon *The Friends of Emily Culpepper* by Ann Coleridge and Roland Harvey.

Case study: *The Friends of Emily Culpepper*

The book is about a sweet looking old lady who makes people who visit her house, like the milkman and the policeman, small and keeps them in jars. She lets them out to play but returns them to the jars at the end of the day.

A class of 8–9-year-olds decided to hold villagers' meetings each day for two weeks to discuss what they should do about Emily. Each day the class chose a chair for the meeting and other members of the class chose to play characters either directly from the book like Emily or relatives of the characters or other interested local people like a newspaper reporter. The teacher acted purely as a secretary to the meetings and they were always chaired by one of the class, though a different member for each meeting (see Figure 4.4). The only preparation the children needed to start the activity after hearing the story was a brief introduction to how meetings operated and how to indicate that they wanted to say something in this situation. The activity started because of interest created by the story and lasted about two weeks before the interest waned and the meetings came to a natural conclusion. What is important here is that the idea came from the children and the teacher allowed this activity to become part of the daily routine of the class as meetings were always held first thing in the morning. Children would often come into school having considered ideas to raise in the morning meetings and the class dictated the direction and the topics to be discussed.

Third Villagers meeting.

Heather was our reporter and chairlady.
The meeting started with moans and groans about what Emily had been doing.

Kenny - get the policeman
Jacob - take a vote
Andrea - set a trap

Kenny agreed with Jacob about a vote.
Terry was the only one who didn't agree but couldn't say why.
Suggestions came from the floor to be voted on as follows:

Third Villagers meeting (continued) 3
Suggestions   Votes

1/ Take her to prison ,   0
2/ Get the police .   0
3/ Set a trap for her.   0
4/ Steal her potion .   0
5/ Put stuff in her food.   0
6/ Change the potion in the
   bottle for wine   1
7/ Talk to Emily   0
8/ Get her a pen-pal   25
   (to stop her feeling lonely)
9/ All the people who deliver
   things to Emily should put
   them in a box.   1
                                    No votes 1
                                    Absences 3

Suggestion 8 is the winner

Third Meeting (continued).   3
Having decided on what to do with Emily the villagers are going to meet again tomorrow to put their suggestion to Emily.

Figure 4.4 Extract from villagers' meeting notes

 Curriculum links

The skills used in this case study could include thinking, speaking including clearly articulating ideas in whole class discussion, listening, negotiating and dealing with disagreement, empathy, problem solving, chairing, role play and others depending upon the level of engagement and participation.

Exploratory play

Many learning opportunities lend themselves to exploratory play. In this example, an old suitcase with artefacts from a trip abroad is the hook for this play idea. The idea behind this specific activity is that a group explores the artefacts and develops a story of the trip taken by the owner of the suitcase over the period of a week. For older children artefacts can include timetables, tickets for travel, and to see particular sights, payment for meals in specific locations, souvenirs from the places visited and photographs, plus items of clothing and other equipment that might give some clues to the kinds of activities undertaken during the trip. The children can be given the opportunity to investigate the contents of the case and each of the items, and to research using the internet, maps and other resources in order to explore the locations and establish a plan for the suitcase owner's visit.

 Case study: A holiday suitcase

As a starter for the class of 6–7-year-olds about to start learning about Chinese New Year, one Friday afternoon before a holiday period they bade farewell to their class toy, Harold, who was going on a mystery vacation. After the two-week break the children were very excited and curious to see where Harold had been on his holiday. However, on arriving at school their class teacher explained how he had received an email from Harold saying that his plane had been delayed but he attached a photograph from his holiday. The attachment, shown on the class interactive whiteboard (IWB) was a photo of Harold on a very large concrete structure (a picture of the Great Wall of China with Harold cleverly inserted by his teacher using Photoshop). Discussion about where he might have been on holiday ensued. Shortly after the discussion began, the school administrator entered the room explaining that she had received a phone call from Harold saying he was on his way and that she would bring him in when he returned.

The class teacher took the opportunity in the intervening period to settle the children into a circle and to talk to them about Harold's suitcase, how it would contain clues about where he had been on holiday and about asking questions about the clues.

On Harold's entry to the classroom a child was chosen to remove one item from the suitcase and the children were encouraged to talk with their 'talk partner' about the object. After a short time the children asked one question about the item to Harold, who whispered the answer to their teacher, who in turn relayed the answer. This continued for a number of items until the children had enough clues about Harold's suitcase to make the decision that he had been to China on holiday. The session continued with play that involved the children choosing which item they would learn about further.

Curriculum links

The skills used in this idea could include turn taking, asking questions, and problem solving. Older children could also use geographical enquiry, research, currency conversion, language translation, map reading, reading timetables, time zone calculations and others depending upon the route through the investigation.

Games play

Games play is probably the most common type of play used throughout the primary age range. This is because games activities are a statutory part of most national curricula for physical education.

 Case study: Ultimate dodgeball

A whole primary school decided to get involved in the British Heart Foundation's (BHF) fundraising event called Ultimate Dodgeball (see www.bhf.org.uk/get-involved/events/schools-and-youth-groups/ultimate-dodgeball.aspx). Each child was given a sponsorship form to encourage them to raise funds. Dodgeball competitions were held in the school hall between children from parallel classes (two classes of 30 of the same age group). The finals were held on a day when the children were encouraged to dress up in a creative way. For example, one team of 10–11-year-olds dressed up as nurses and another team of 7–8-year-olds were dressed and had their faces painted as cats. All children who got involved received a participation certificate and those who won each year group's competition received a medal.

The tournament was held over a period of several weeks to support the development of dodgeball skills (catching, throwing and dodging a ball), to encourage as much participation as possible, to give the children time to creatively prepare for the final, and to learn as much as possible about the BHF, their work and the need to keep healthy and active.

 Curriculum links

The skills used in this idea could include team work, developing strategy, using tactics and skills suitable for attacking and defending, evaluating and improving performance, as well as knowledge and understanding of fitness and health.

Integrated play

Meaningful links can be made between two or more curriculum subjects (Fogarty and Pete, 2007). This case study demonstrates how Sarah, a trainee teacher on her final placement, used a design and technology unit to help the children to understand more about life as an ancient Greek person.

 Case study: Greek sandals

Sarah writes about her planning, teaching and assessment in a joint history and design and technology unit for 10–11-year-old children.

'This topic took place in the first half term of January in a large, generally higher ability Year 6 class in a village school. The class had begun to learn about modern Greece in the first half of the six-week term, and then this moved to looking at ancient Greece, their cultures and general knowledge.

'So, I decided to use design technology to increase their understanding of ancient Greece further. I felt that art was an area they had already covered in relation to ancient Greeks lower down in school from past experience, and thought that they would enjoy the challenge of a more practical lesson to learn about the Greeks.

'We began by learning about where sandals originated, who they were made for and how sandals represented who you were in society. We looked at a range of images from the time as well as of recreated sandals now, and also looked at some modern Greek-styled fashion sandals. I did a very quick and basic modelling of the paper prototype showing the class how to draw around their feet to make sure the sandal was the right size and then put two basic straps across the top of the foot to show that designs could be as simple or as elaborate as they wanted. From this the children began to design their own considering a range of different elements, including practicality, durability, appearance, cost, materials and construction. We made an idea bank of different things we would have to be aware of and then decided on the best materials for the designs. For example, cotton material was suggested to make the straps with as this is comfortable, but other children suggested that cotton is not as strong as other materials, and may fray when cutting therefore making the product untidy. We also spoke about items which would be available for us to use, for instance the school didn't have glue guns so we had to find different methods to create joins. The children drew a picture of their design, and then made a paper prototype. From this we were able to explore practicality more and understand if our designs would work or be too impractical or complicated.

'In the lesson where the sandals were made we discussed waste of materials. In hindsight this could have been improved by linking it to the current maths

(Continued)

(Continued)

topic of measures. We could have begun to measure accurately, discuss standard and non-standard units of measurement, area, and appropriate units of length for the purpose of the task; this would have also reduced waste as the class would know exactly what they needed as they would have already measured it out.

'During construction we discussed in mini-plenaries tips to use to provide a good finish, including trimming wadding under the insole section to make it neater. We also talked about joining the straps and how to make it neater by trying to hide the staples. Another area which arose was how to make the sandals practical. The class decided that many of their designs would have to include fasteners to allow the foot to fit into the sandal, while others decided that although their product was visually appealing, it was impractical to wear due to the materials used (for example, butterfly clips for decoration would be sharp on the foot).

'In the final session the children evaluated the sandals, discussing what was effective, what didn't work, what they would or could improve, and also reconsidered the design elements (durability, appearance, practicality, etc.) and talked about which ones were levant to their designs. The class realised we had made another version of a prototype, that in most cases was impractical to wear. This led to more evaluation of how we could make a wearable product in the future. In the evaluation we also linked back to the historical elements and talked about whether the sandal would be suitable for the climate in Greece, where we designed our sandals for. The children could tell from the sandal the sort of person who would wear it, for example, highly embellished sandals would be for the rich because they could afford it.'

 Curriculum links

The skills used in this idea could include historical interpretation, historical enquiry, and knowledge and understanding of people and changes in the past. In relation to design and technology, the children could develop, plan and communicate ideas, work with tools, equipment, materials and components to make quality products, and evaluate processes and products.

Play involving the whole school environment and beyond

Play activities do not have to be restricted to the classroom space and working on a large scale can support the development of visualisation skills. It also makes the play physically active and makes use of the whole school environment.

Case study: Dinosaurs

A class of 8–10-year-old children were involved in a four-week theme related to dinosaurs. One mathematics lesson involved the children working in small groups using the large school field to estimate the length of dinosaurs. The group were given a number of pictures of dinosaurs with the length of the dinosaur in centimetres or metres. Their task was to order the lengths of the dinosaurs from shortest to longest placing the pictures (on lolly sticks) into the ground. After completing the task, the children were allowed to choose one length to measure accurately with a tape measure. Any adjustments to estimations could be made, before final checks were carried out by the children. The children discussed their findings outside and on their return to the classroom.

Figure 4.5   Dinosaur length estimation

Later in the unit a visiting road show arrived with an inflatable Tyrannosaurus Rex which was erected in the school grounds. Despite their earlier work the children were still surprised that all 36 children and their teachers could stand comfortably under the belly of the animal between its legs!

 ## Curriculum links

The skills used in this idea could include estimation of length and measurement centimetre or metre conversion, team work, collaboration, visualisation, problem solving, mathematical discussion and adaptation (scientific thinking).

Replication play

Replication play is linked to role play as it allows children to experience roles that they are unfamiliar with or are familiar with from a different perspective. This is increasingly used to build empathy and social understanding but it can also be a powerful way to contextualise specific subject knowledge as can be seen in the example that follows.

 Case study: Roman legionnaires

As part of an invaders and settlers history project there were opportunities for two classes of 7–9-year-olds to replicate some of the activities of roman legionnaires in order to gain a more holistic view of their lives. The first was to equip themselves with all the necessary items for each of the soldiers. Figure 4.6 shows an activity sheet the children were required to use to equip themselves.

The basic equipment was:

- Cassis – helmet

  Measure around the head of one person in the group. Measure the circumference of their head. Can you work out what the length is in uncial (inches) or pes (feet) or both?
  1 uncia is 24.6mm and 1 pes is 296mm

- Lorica Segmentata – armour

- Focale and cingulum – scarf and tunic worn under armour

- Gladius – sword, 24 inches long
  I inch or uncia = 24.6 mm
  Draw out a sword the right length for your soldier

- Pilium – medium-length throwing spear 6 feet long
  1 pes is 296mm
  Draw out a spear the right length for your soldier

- Scutum – shield

- Red battle cloak

- Sandals

Draw around both feet of one person in the group. Measure the length of the feet. Can you work out what the length is in uncia (inches) or pes (feet) or both?
1 uncia is 24.6mm and 1 pes is 296mm

Figure 4.6   Roman legionnaire's equipment

Another task was to think about the weight of a full kit. Figure 4.7 presents another activity the children were involved in.

For everything a soldier would carry the full weight would be 60–80 pounds. One libra or pound = 327.2g. Can you put weights in the bag so that it has about the right weight for a soldier to carry?

Roman measures

One uncia is 24.6mm

One pes is 296mm

One cubitus or cubit = 444mm

One gradus or step = 0.74m

One passus or pace = 1.48m

Can you use these measures to measure things in the classroom?

Find out how far it is around the playground in a Roman measure.

A Roman soldier would be expected to walk 20 miles a day. One milliarium or mile is 1.48km. How many times around the playground would the soldier be expected to walk in a day?

Figure 4.7   The weight of a full kit

 Curriculum links

The skills used in this idea could include measuring, conversion, estimating and countering.

Small world play

Model villages or railways are often a short distance from main towns and cities. They can be used to explore small world play as this case study demonstrates.

 Case study: A visit to Madurodam

As part of a week-long school excursion to Holland, a group of forty English 10–11-year-old children visited Madurodam (see www.madurodam.com/en) for half a day. The model village showcases a number of Dutch scenes such as canals, houses, windmills, an airport, a railway system and the like all to a scale of 1:25.

(Continued)

(Continued)

The children toured the village in small groups accompanied by an adult and were free to choose their route and direction of investigation. For example, one group chose to research Dutch hydraulic engineering projects following the water route (available at http://www.madurodam.com/files/documents/Route%20 Water_EN.pdf).

The teacher had planned to use the visit to Madurodam as a springboard for the children to explore scale and ratio further on their return to school. However, when explaining this to them, the children quickly informed her that her idea (of the children recreating their bedrooms to scale) had been done last year and that they wanted to create something along the lines of Madurodam based on their school. They wanted to recreate their school in the school hall and ask parents for a donation to view it. The funds would then be donated to a youth-orientated charity just as the profit from Madurodam is today.

The children initially chose a scale of 1:100 because they felt it was an easier scale factor but they quickly decided that it would make construction of many of the items in the playground too difficult. So the scale of 1:50 was agreed upon. Using digital cameras the children took photographs of objects and used these printed out to an approximate scale to help them to construct their model school. The final product was so warmly welcomed by parents that the local

Figure 4.8   Madurodam

press also became involved and the school opened its model to the public for two days after publicity in the local paper and on the radio station, raising more money than the children ever imagined.

 Curriculum links

The skills used in this idea could include calculations involving division and fractions, measurement and money.

Role play

As we have mentioned earlier, taking on a role is linked to replication play and can be used to build empathy and social understanding. It also offers opportunities to practise skills and knowledge in a specific and safe context, as in the case study which follows.

Case study: The French cafe

Learning a foreign language has increased in primary schools and a key skill is practising how to actually say what you want in another language. The National Strategy for MFL in Key Stage 2 focuses on skills:

- to ensure an early start towards competence in a foreign language
- to develop language learning skills that can be transferred to any language
- to broaden linguistic awareness, extending literacy beyond English
- to develop cultural knowledge and awareness, extending children's horizons.

Playing roles of a shop keeper in a bakery and using French, Spanish or German as the spoken medium offers a good rationale for structured role play for children to develop spoken language skills. In the case study below we can see how intercultural awareness is developed.

> Developing cultural awareness is an integral part of learning another language. From the earliest stages of learning a new language, children can learn about the countries and communities where the language is spoken, their culture, traditions and way of life. Although the main focus may be on developing children's knowledge, skills and understanding in the new language, schemes of work should cover cultural aspects of the language studied and, where appropriate, different ethnic groups among native speakers. (DfES, 2007: 46)

Case study: At a restaurant

This case study shares the work of a trainee teacher who is an MFL specialist. Helen, teaching in a class of 8–10-year-old children, used role play activities that developed the children's understanding of French.

Before school, Helen set up the school hall to look like a French cafe, including playing French music and putting French posters on the walls. Menus were placed on the tables. After the register was taken, Helen assumed the role of a maître dè and informed the children that they would be customers in the cafe, or waiters and waitresses. The children practised ordering food for their petit dejeuner (breakfast), for example, 'Je voudrais un croissant, s'il vous plaît.' Once confident, the 'customers' moved to the cafe, and the waiters/waitresses were given jackets to wear and pads to take orders. Croissants, pains au chocolat and brioche were served alongside jus d'orange and chocolat. The children were encouraged to dunk their food into the hot chocolate.

Helen explains, 'Although it took a little longer to set up, this lesson helped the children to become more confident in using the French sentences they'd been practising for a while in class. My earlier evaluations show that some of the children didn't seem to be as focused as I'd have liked and I thought that the practice in the class was a little removed from reality. Those children who had been less motivated earlier were really keen to be involved and they spoke a lot more French than they normally would. I thought the context helped them to develop their cultural knowledge and awareness further. They enjoyed dipping their breakfasts into the hot chocolate, and some of the children had not tried the French food or hot chocolate before.'

Curriculum links

The skills used in this idea could include oracy, literacy and intercultural understanding from the Languages Framework. It could also involve team working and speaking and listening skills.

Virtual play

Virtual Learning Environments (VLEs) are growing in popularity in primary schools. Although there is currently no formal or peer-reviewed evaluation of their effectiveness, in the case study below Miles Berry (2005) writes about his own experiences of piloting a VLE as a teacher in a preparatory school for 3–11-year-olds.

Case study: Using virtual learning environments (VLEs)

Berry identifies the following benefits of using a VLE to support a class of 9–11 year olds' mathematics homework.

- The children valued the instant feedback from online assessment.
- Help was readily accessible from peers or the teacher through discussion forums. This appeared to make the children more confident to discuss mathematics.
- Children who were shy in class exhibited no such shyness online.
- Children valued the opportunity to return to previous work to review it, particularly if they were absent from class.
- Children who were not able to attend school were often able to engage in the learning from elsewhere.
- The pilot year children obtained the school's highest ever SATs results in mathematics.

Curriculum links

The skills used in this idea could include exchanging and sharing information, reviewing, modifying and evaluating work as it progresses, working with a range of information, working with others, as well as investigating uses of ICT inside and outside school.

Summary

This chapter has provided one illustration of each of the types of play we discussed in Chapter 3. Consider the implications for your own practice by reflecting on the following questions.

1 Which case studies did you feel most excited by? Reflect on what made you feel this way.
2 Were there any case studies that you felt you would not be able to achieve in your current situation? Note down which inhibiting factors you could change and decide what your next steps could be to address those.
3 What is the very next step you are going to take in order to have a go at implementing a type of play you have not yet planned and facilitated or that you want to develop further?
4 Who can you approach about supporting you along the way to implementing your new idea?

Further reading 📖

Read more about making your own village using free downloadable software at www.yourchildlearns.com/vill_act.htm

Moodle is an open-source VLE. Find out more about Moodle at http://moodle.org/

References

Berry, M. (2005) 'A virtual learning environment in primary education'. Available at: www.worldecitizens.net/ftp/Primary%20VLE.pdf (accessed July 2011).

DfES (2007) *The Key Stage 2 Framework for Languages.* London: National Strategies, Reference: DFES 1721 2005.

Fogarty, R. and Pete, B.M. (2007) *How to Integrate the Curricula,* 3rd edn. London: Sage Publications.

CHAPTER 5

THE ROLE OF THE TEACHER AND OTHER ADULTS IN PLAY

Introduction

Teachers and other adults have numerous roles in different types of play-based learning. This chapter will explore the complexity of these roles. In doing so, it will not give a 'one size fits all' guide to the roles because all learners approach play-based learning differently and all teachers and other adults have their own interpretation of what play-based learning looks like in the classroom. Instead, the chapter explores a number of ways of conceiving the roles of adults and children and invites you to consider which ways will work for you in your situation.

Control, power and ownership in play

At a general level, adults' roles are fairly clear. For example, teachers and other adults in school are perceived by children and colleagues as what is deemed as being 'professional'. Although this may also be interpreted in a number of ways, within this role teachers are not playmates or conversational peers (Kernan, 2007). However, some researchers state that in a play-orientated curriculum there is a shift of focus of power: the locus of control is with the children and not the adult (Brown and Freeman, 2001; Wood and Attfield, 2005). This may cause concern to teachers. For example, Forbes and McCloughan (2010) found that an investigative play approach successfully engaged primary school children in quality scientific investigations because they were decision makers and became confident learners. At first the teachers were concerned about this way of working but after a time they valued the experience of working alongside their pupils because they found it supported their professional learning. In the article, one teacher reflects on this way of working.

> I think that it's a bit frightening at first. At first we felt that we weren't delivering these outcomes. *We thought they were just playing* but then we realised, 'no', by the time you're working yourself through it you realise how much they've learnt and how much they've got out of it. (Our italics) (2010: 28)

It may be helpful to know that even in an established play-based learning environment such as the EYFS there is still confusion over the teacher's role. 'However, there remains some confusion about how to interpret the EYFS requirement for planned, purposeful play' (Tickell, 2011: Para 3.33). In this section we discuss how to address the potential issues of control, power and ownership in play in the primary school.

In Chapter 1 we introduced the planning paradox, where:

> Play can facilitate learning and so there is a desire to incorporate play-like freedom into more formal school-based learning, even for older pupils. However, such a strategy transfers control over what is learned away from the teacher to the pupils themselves. This is unsatisfactory if the teacher has an agenda in which certain specific knowledge should be assimilated. (Ainley et al., 2006: 23)

Here, Ainley et al. identify two issues within the paradox: the notion of 'control' and 'agendas'. We take these together. After all, it is the agenda that drives and controls the actions.

A Piagetian view of play would suggest that children learn by exploring and discovering and it should be their agenda that drives their learning. Following this approach means that adults should have minimal intervention in their play and that the teachers' role should be as a 'stage manager'. However, in the primary school children are less involved in this type of play and we often observe directed activity where it is the teacher's agenda leading the way. In the following section we discuss thinking about play according to power, control and agenda.

Thinking about play according to balance of adult/child input and initiation

Three common categorisations of play are:

- *Child-led*: influenced by the context the child is in, including resources and other children available to them (sometimes called 'free' or 'independent' play)
- *Structured/guided*: resources are intentionally controlled; adult has a clear learning outcome; any adult intervention is guided by these learning outcomes
- *Adult-led*: reduced choices for child; adult's agenda.

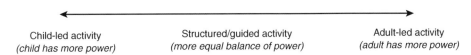

Figure 5.1 The play and power continuum

These can be considered part of a play and power continuum (see Figure 5.1).

What is potentially dangerous in the ideas above and in the play paradox is that the approaches to play are seen as an either/or model. If learning is conceived in this way, then striking an appropriate balance between the two is no doubt difficult. Although speaking within an early years context, Tickell perhaps offers a way forward:

> I ... believe that it is not possible to separate out child-initiated from adult-guided or directed [adult-led] learning. When working with young children, the exchange between adults and children should be fluid, moving interchangeably between activities initiated by children and adult responses helps build the child's learning and understanding. (2011: Para 3.33)

The way adults intervene (and know when not to intervene) in children's play is crucial to the success of a play-based approach to learning. Indeed, when an adult or more experienced peer intervenes, there is opportunity for activities in the child's Zone of Proximal Development (ZPD) (Vygotsky, 1978) to be performed. Scaffolding (Bruner, 1978) children's learning helps to develop their academic, emotional and social development (Sepulveda et al., 2011).

It is possible to see in Figure 5.2 that in this way of conceptualising play, adult ownership and power remain inversely proportionate to child ownership and power, but movement around the grid should be fluid.

Dockett and Fleer (1999) suggest three roles of adults in play-based learning environments. As a *manager*, the adult manages the resources, time and space. This would also include being aware of risks such as checking equipment and internet safety. As a *facilitator*, the adult mediates, promotes equity and interprets children's play. As a *player*, the adult engages with the children in parallel play, co-playing and play tutoring. This may be a useful way to engage children who are finding it more difficult to become involved in the learning opportunity. With these three roles come different types of responsibility.

Seeing these roles in the light of Tickell's comment about fluidity, we represent Dockett and Fleer's model in an alternative way (Figure 5.3). We have intentionally placed the child-led activity at the centre to

- reflect the principle of child as autonomous learner
- remind ourselves that every child should be the focus of the learning
- stress that the child is the active participant in learning who constructs their own knowledge and understanding.

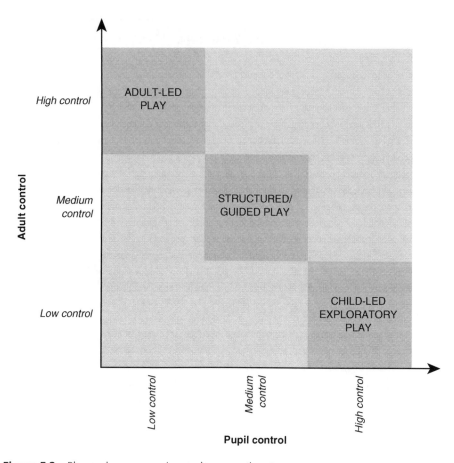

Figure 5.2   Play and power are inversely proportionate

▦ Activity

Consider the types of play below that were introduced in Chapter 3.

- artistic or design play
- controlled imaginary play/social dramatic play
- exploratory play
- games play
- integrated play
- play using the whole school environment and beyond
- replication play
- role play
- small world play
- virtual play.

As you will have seen earlier, each type of play will be played out differently in different contexts. However, reflect upon a time you used one of these approaches or imagine yourself using one of these approaches. Think about the roles you took on. Where in Figures 5.1, 5.2 or 5.3 could you have placed yourself? What were you doing at that time? What principles (see Chapter 2) were you following at the time? Can you now move yourself to another part of the model? Why/why not? What could you do differently to improve the learning experience for the children?

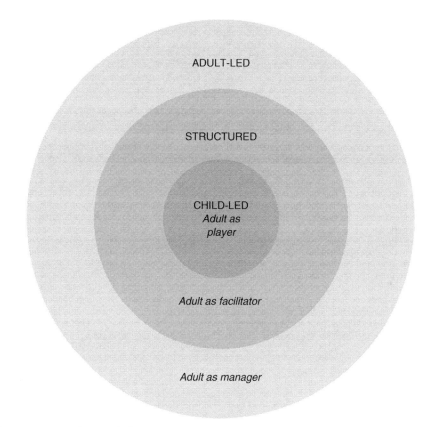

Figure 5.3   Dockett and Fleer's adult roles within a play-based environment

When to intervene and not to intervene

We believe that it is a priority for adults in the class to value play and it is important to demonstrate this through appropriate intervention during play-based learning. Chapter 6 discusses further how a learning environment can be set up to reflect the play-based approach to learning. Many researchers believe that children learn to be playful from their parents and other influential adults (Berk and Winsler, 1995).

   Before intervening, it is useful to pause and to think about your intentions for intervention. What is your agenda? Why are you wanting to intervene? Of course if a situation is dangerous you must intervene immediately. However, there are many other reasons for intervening including sustaining and enriching the play, challenging and helping to extend the play, as a mediator, to adapt the environment, to assess the children (see Chapter 7), to enter peer play, to support children's entry and exit in the play, to scaffold learning and to advocate (Bruce, 1996; Dockett and Fleer, 2002; Jones and Reynolds, 1992).

How to intervene

Your intervention should be well matched and appropriate for the children. Although teachers thought that their intervention was appropriate, Bennett et al. found that teachers often did not intervene, because the children had already met the learning outcome of the activity, or the teacher observed behaviours that the children were exhibiting and therefore did not intervene to challenge or extend their learning, or sometimes children were focused on an aspect that was not related to the teacher's learning outcome (1997: 73).

When you intervene, what do you focus upon? Will the intervention be academically focused, or will it be to develop the children's interpersonal skills? Are you going to tell, model, or elicit from the children? Will it be a combination of these?

Siraj-Blatchford (2004, 2007) found that the characteristics of intervention that led to positive outcomes for 3–7-year-old children include:

- adult and child involvement
- cognitive (co-constructive) engagement and sustained shared thinking between adults and children
- the use of instruction techniques such as modelling and demonstration, explanation and questioning.

Parents and play

A significant group of adults to involve in planning and learning is parents. This section will explore two aspects related to parents. The first is parents' perceptions of play and the second is involving parents in play-based learning. Please note that 'parents' is used throughout but should be read as parents/caregivers as well as other family members such as older siblings, uncles and aunts, or grandparents.

Parents' perceptions of play

Just as theorists, practitioners and teachers have different perceptions of play, so do parents. In their large-scale study of parents' and experts' (child development professionals) perceptions of play, Fisher et al. (2008) found that parents' and experts' perceptions of play do differ in their conceptualisation and values about play. It showed that parents define play more broadly than experts. Parents attributed more learning value to structured play whereas experts associated less learning value to these activities compared to unstructured activities. If this is the case more generally, then teachers and schools may have a duty to work with parents to develop a shared ethos of the play-based approaches to learning the school has adopted.

Often parental expectations have been blamed for downward pressure on the curriculum (Elkind, 2007; Hayes, 2006; Weikart, 1999), and when first implementing a play-based approach to learning parental resistance may be found (Souto-Manning and Lee 2005). Souto-Monning and Lee undertook an investigative approach that required children research their own question, or learn more about particular topics. This reflects our principles for play-based learning specifically in relation to autonomous, investigative, problem-solving and reflective learners. Souto-Manning and Lee found that after initial resistance (for example, Parent: 'In the beginning I thought it was all about play' (2005: 9); 'At first I thought it was all too much for [children that age]' (2005: 16)) parents' perceptions changed to 'overwhelmingly positive reactions' (2005: 14). An analysis of their comments revealed:

- increased motivation of their children to learn (and this curbed poor behaviour)
- the building of a community of learners (that included special educational needs (SEN), EAL and gifted and talented children)
- utilising children's strengths (individuals were valued for the part they played in the collaborative work)
- improved academic achievement
- encouraging parental involvement (where parents were learning with their children).

Involving parents in play

 Points for reflection

Reflect on the schools you have been involved with. What is their attitude to parental involvement? Do they have an inviting climate for parents?

Research (Zhao and Akiba, 2009) identifies that attitude and climate influence parents' decisions in becoming involved in school life. This is reflected in Harris and Goodall's UK research that showed how 'schools rather than parents are often hard to reach' (2008: 277). Harris and Goodall also identified that different strategies are required to engage a diverse range of parents. Indeed, parents bring a wide-ranging skill set and knowledge base about a plethora of domains. 'Involving parents in school activities has an important social and community function' (Harris and Goodall, 2008: 277). Parents will willingly give their time and resources for free if they feel welcomed and valued in what they are doing to support their child and their peers.

Table 5.1 Support from older family members

Case study	Curriculum subjects this related to
A neighbour of a child's grandparents came to speak about being a children's author. He read them a story and talked to them about how he became an author and shared tips for writing with them. He also talked to them about the importance of illustrations in picture books and about who he worked with to produce these.	English (writing, reading); art and design (illustrations)
A father invited the children in the class to his pub. He explained the rules of pool including the scoring and showed them how to hold a cue. He explained the importance of using chalk on the cue and how to use angle to pocket the balls. The children then played their own games of pool on the tables.	Mathematics (angle, number); science (materials and their properties)
A father brought in a working motor so that the class could see how cams worked.	Science; design and technology
Two classes were learning about the Second World War and they had a morning where they were role playing being evacuated. A grandmother of one of the children's friends visited their 'shelter' and answered questions about what it was like being a child during the war, including having to live with a family in Wales after being evacuated from Liverpool.	History; Personal Social Health & Economic (PSHE) education
An uncle who worked for a world-wide map-making company spoke to the class about how his job involved taking treks all over the world to check the accuracy of their maps. He brought in artefacts from the country they were currently studying. He also talked about the impact that Global Positioning Systems were having on the company and how his job was changing because of this.	Geography; ICT
A mother brought in her patchwork quilts and showed the children how she designed them and produced them. She talked about the shapes and patterns in the quilts.	Art and design; mathematics (shape and space)
An older cousin joined the class during his work experience fortnight. He annotated the compositions that the children sung him and accompanied a class assembly where they were sung.	Music (composition); English (lyrics)
An uncle of one of the children visited to tell them about his involvement in two Commonwealth Games in rowing. He talked about training, the location and political context of the games, his feelings about being in the competition and in the closing ceremonies.	Physical education (team work); history; PSHE

Table 5.1 provides authentic examples of how family members visited a class to provide a supporting or motivating role for curriculum subjects. Note: All case studies also present opportunities for speaking and listening.

The sheet in Figure 5.4 provides an example of a form you could send to the parents of the children in your class after go-ahead from your head teacher.

 Activity

Think about a subject that you have recently taught. How could you have used a parent to support or enhance what you were doing?

> Dear Parents and caregivers
>
> Welcome to Class 2 for this academic year. As you know, our school develops active links with parents in many different ways including open days, inviting parents to be involved in school educational visits, and helping in other classrooms to read with children or participate in other regular activities.
>
> In addition to this, I'd like to hear what skills and interests you, or other adults in your extended family, have that you may be willing to share with the children during the year. For example, last year we had a mum who came in to share with the class how she cooked Dal Rasam, a South Indian soup dish. An aunt shared her postcard collection for a local history project. One father brought his Backhoe Loader tractor in for the children to learn about! What do you think you could offer? From experience we know every child in the class knows someone who has something to share!
>
> Please could you complete the form below and return it to school by the end of next week. Please use additional paper if you require it!
>
> Thank you for your ongoing support.
>
> --
>
> Adult's name: _____
>
> Relationship to child: _____ Child from Class 2's name: _____
>
> I would be able to share the following skills/interests/knowledge with the children:
>
> I am best contacted in the following way: _____
>
> Signed: _____ Date: _____

Figure 5.4 Example of a newsletter asking for parental involvement

Involving other adults

In addition to parents and other family members there are many other adults who have specific expertise to support particular work you are doing in your school or classroom. In the case study below we meet a creative practitioner who worked with the teachers to develop a play-based approach to learning with the older children in the school. In Chapter 9 we will present a case study of another creative practitioner visiting Dallas Road School to work with selected children to produce a centenary mural.

 Case study: 'Creating a museum of change' – Croftlands Junior School, Ulverston

Croftlands Junior School is a six-class school of 7–11-year-old children in Ulverston, Cumbria. There are three classes of 7–9-year-old children in the lower school and three classes of 9–11-year-old children in the upper school. As part of its school improvement plan, the staff at Croftlands Junior School worked with Creative Partnerships to develop the way they approach learning and teaching. With Hank,

(Continued)

(Continued)

a Creative Practitioner funded through the Creative Partnerships programme, the staff planned and implemented a project they called 'The Museum of Change'.

Introduction to the project

The project used the concept of 'change' as an anchor for the children's learning.

- The project was designed to be a fixed-term 'one-off' activity.
- On average three to four half-day sessions per week for one term allowed children to undertake their research.
- It offered the children the opportunity to choose their own topic to research in relation to change (topics included, for example, hospitals, Lego, fashion, war and planes).
- The children had free choice over the focus of their research, the method of their research, how they presented their findings and in some cases who they worked with.
- The project culminated in an assembly and a school-wide 'museum of change' where the children shared their findings with parents and governors.

The project was evaluated by the staff during a day-long meeting facilitated by Hank. The intention of the review meeting was to identify successes and challenges of the project's approach and to identify what might usefully be taken forward into future planning and implementation of the curriculum.

Key aspects and issues from the project

During the staff review of the project the following key aspects and issues were identified and discussed:

- The relatively recently appointed head teacher had a clear vision for how the children's learning opportunities could improve.

  Headteacher: 'This is a big shift for the school. The timetable was very subject-driven. We're freeing everything up and the staff are becoming more skilled in working this way.'

- The staff fully embraced the project although they found it difficult at first to believe that they could facilitate it and that the children would work effectively.

  Teacher: 'At first I just wanted [Hank] to tell us what to do. Our working practice has been like that for so long.'

- Before the project began they developed a series of groundrules for the project's approach to teaching and learning. They worked to remain true to those groundrules throughout, although it was difficult at times.

  Teacher: 'We normally have objectives we have to cover. It was a really worrying change but in the end it was OK because the children did what they did and it was good.'

  Teacher: 'I said to them "It's your topic and your choice and I'm finding it hard too". ... I felt very in their hands.'

- A distinction was made between the types of outcomes encountered which could be categorised into process-orientated and product-orientated outcomes. Process-oriented outcomes included decision making, group working, the editing process to make their findings audience-ready, research skills, and self-management of learning.
- More outcomes were process-orientated than product-orientated and this was difficult for most of the teachers to feel comfortable with.

  Teacher: 'They would have a 30 or 40 minute lesson on the internet and may not have found anything useful.'

- The teachers identified significant impact for the children.

  A higher level of engagement from all children. 'They [the children] don't see us as having control, they see themselves as in control.'

  One teacher used 'two stars and a wish' to evidence the impact on her children. Some comments:

Stars	Wishes
• Helping other people with their books	• I wish I can do more like this
• Making new friends	• Some of us would have liked more adult support than others
• I like being the boss of what I'm doing	• Next time I would like to decide how we present our work
• I'm not relying on Mrs G as much as I'm more confident working like this	
• Having a choice	

- Some children struggled with the approach used in the project but the teachers were confident that they would be able to support the children more effectively in the future.

  Teacher: 'It is not going to suit everybody just as another way won't suit everybody.'

  Teacher: 'If we're doing more I'd think about supporting those children. I know what I could put in.'

  Teacher: 'All the way through school they've been told what to do and how to do it. We can't expect it to be fantastic as a one-off.'

The teachers' roles

The teachers significantly re-evaluated their roles. On a general level they reassessed their own purpose and motivation for being teachers (Teachers: 'It is all about them, not us'; 'It has been a fundamental shift [in our thinking and the way we do things'; 'The children were capable of much more than I thought and I need to trust them more').

Furthermore, the teachers reassessed their own perception of the National Curriculum requirements and curriculum content (Teacher 1: 'In fact we don't

(Continued)

(Continued)

have to teach "mountains" next term, that is what the QCDA [schemes of work] said we had to do. The National Curriculum is telling us we have to focus on geographical enquiry'). This impacted upon the way they are going to plan in the future, giving more control over planning to the children.

Conclusion

A key factor in the success of this project was that the head teacher provided the opportunity and permission to trial a completely radical way of working, facilitated by the Creative Partnerships Practitioner. The project was never intended to be repeated within the school. Instead, not only have the children developed their learning skills, but the teachers have learnt a lot through undertaking the process. This process has challenged their perspectives of learning and teaching and their roles within this and they look forward to continuing to develop their school curriculum further. Staff have already identified ways in which they can incorporate the principles of giving children more choice in the learning process into the next topics they will be teaching.

How to find other adults to help

Word of mouth is often a highly effective way to find quality people to work with your school and your children. However, if this has not been successful for you then there are other places you can search. The list below provides a starting point and it is by no means exhaustive.

- The *National Literacy Trust* has produced a document 'Involving organisations and adults from the community' available at www.literacytrust.org.uk/assets/0000/7716/Involving_organisations_and_adults_from_the_wider_community.pdf to help you with reading projects.
- *Creative practitioners directories* such as the one at Northamptonshire County Council's website www.northamptonshire.gov.uk/en/councilservices/leisure/arts/arted/tss/pages/artists.aspx provide networking opportunities for schools to meet potential providers.
- Providers such as Curious Minds www.curiousminds.org.uk/creativepartnerships) facilitate collaborative opportunities to learn creatively.
- *Museums* and *archives* (various) may offer opportunities for adults with various skills and knowledge to support school activities.
- Liaising with *secondary schools* and *initial teacher training providers* may also provide assistance from older children and young adults who have developed an area of interest and expertise in that area. (See case study in Chapter 9 for more on working with secondary schools.)

Summary

Reflect upon your own practice by thinking about the following questions in relation to play activities.

1 What is your interpretation of play in the primary curriculum at this stage of reading this book?
2 What evidence can you see of your interpretation in practice in your classroom? Can it be observed in the ethos? Is it related to the layout of the room?
3 How do the expectations of play-based activities differ between yourself and colleagues, the children, and the parents/carers?

Further reading

Jones, E. and Reynolds, G. (1992) *The Play's the Thing: Teachers' Roles in Children's Play*. New York: Teachers College Press.
Siraj-Blatchford, I. (2004) 'Quality teaching in the early years', in A. Anning, J. Cullen and M. Fleer (eds), *Early Childhood Education: Society and Culture*. London: Sage Publications. pp. 137–48.

References

Ainley J., Pratt, D. and Hansen, A. (2006) 'Connecting engagement and focus in pedagogic task design', *British Educational Research Journal*, 32 (1): 23–38.
Bennett, N., Wood, L. and Rogers, S. (1997) *Teaching Through Play: Teachers' Thinking and Classroom Practice*. Buckingham: Open University Press.
Berk, L. and Winsler, A. (1995) *Scaffolding Children's Learning: Vygotsky and Early Childhood Education*, Volume 7 of NAEYC Research into Practice Series. Washington D.C.: National Association for the Education of Young Children.
Brown, Mac H. and Freeman, N.K. (2001) '"We don't play that way at preschool": the moral and ethical dimensions of controlling children's play', in S. Reifel and Mac H. Brown (eds), *Early Education and Care and Reconceptualising Play – Advances in Early Education and Day Care*, Volume II. Oxford: Elsevier Science, pp. 259–74.
Bruce, T. (1996) *Quality of Play in Early Childhood Education*. London: Hodder and Stoughton.
Bruner, J.S. (1978) 'The role of dialogue in language acquisition' in A. Sinclair, R.J. Jarvelle, and W.J.M. Levelt (eds), *The Child's Concept of Language*. New York: Springer-Verlag.
Dockett, S. and Fleer, M. (1999) *Play and Pedagogy in Early Childhood*. Marrickville NSW: Harcourt Brace.
Dockett, S. and Fleer, M. (2002) *Play and Pedagogy in Early Childhood: Bending the Rules*. Australia: Nelson.

Elkind, D. (2007) *The Hurried Child: Growing Up Too Fast Too Soon,* 25th anniversary edition. New York: Da Capo Lifelong Learning.

Fisher, K.R., Hirsh-Pasek, K., Golinkoff, R.M. And Gryfe, S.G. (2008) 'Conceptual split? Parents' and experts' perceptions of play in the 21st century', *Journal of Applied Developmental Psychology,* 29: 305–16.

Forbes, A. and McCloughan, G. (2010) 'Increasing student participation in science investigations in primary schools: the *MyScience* initiative', *Teaching Science – the Journal of the Australian Science Teachers Association,* 56 (2): 24–30.

Harris, A. and Goodall, J. (2008) 'Do parents know they matter? Engaging all parents in learning', *Educational Research,* 50 (3): 277–89.

Hayes, N. (2006) 'Play as a pedagogical tool in early years education'. Paper presented at the 2nd International Froebel Society Conference, Froebel College of Education, Sion Hill, Blackrock, Dublin, 29 June to 1 July 2006.

Jones, E. and Reynolds, G. (1992) *The Play's the Thing: Teachers' Roles in Children's Play.* New York: Teachers College Press.

Kernan, M. (2007) 'Play as a context for Early Learning and Development', research paper. NCCA. Available at: www.ncca.ie/en/Curriculum_and_Assessment/Early_ Childhood_and_Primary_Education/Early_Childhood_Education/How_Aistear_ was_developed/Research_Papers/Play_paper.pdf (accessed July 2011).

Sepulveda, C., Garza, Y. and Morrison, M.O. (2011) 'Child teacher relationship training: a phenomenological study', *International Journal of Play Therapy,* 20 (1): 12–25.

Siraj-Blatchford, I. (2004) 'Quality teaching in the early years', in A. Anning, J. Cullen and M. Fleer (eds), *Early Childhood Education: Society and Culture.* London: Sage Publications. pp. 137–48.

Siraj-Blatchford, I. (2007) 'Creativity, communication and collaboration: The identification of pedagogic progression in sustained shared thinking', *Asia-Pacific Journal of Research in Early Childhood Education,* 1 (2): 3–23.

Souto-Manning, M. And Lee, K. (2005) '"In the beginning I thought it was all play": perceptions of the project approach in a second grade classroom', *School Community Journal,* 15 (2): 7–20.

Tickell, C. (2011) *The Early Years: Foundations for Life, Health and Learning.* London: Department for Education.

Vygotsky, L.S. (1978) *Mind and Society: The Development of Higher Psychological Processes.* Cambridge, MA: Harvard University Press.

Weikart, D. (ed.) (1999) *What Should Young Children Learn? Teacher and Parent Views in 15 Countries.* The IEA Preprimary Project Phase 2. Ypsilanti, Michigan: High/Scope Press.

Wood, E. and Attfield, J. (2005) *Play, Learning and the Early Childhood Curriculum,* 2nd edn. London: Paul Chapman.

Zhao, H. and Akiba, M. (2009) 'School expectations for parental involvement and student mathematics achievement: a comparative study of middle schools in the US and South Korea', *Compare,* 39 (3): 411–28.

CHAPTER 6

PLANNING FOR PLAY

It is also naïve to think that good play environments can be achieved only through design. (Hart, 2002: 14)

Introduction

In this chapter we look at the issues around planning for play activities with primary aged children and how both adults and children can be involved in the planning and organisation of play environments. It will include discussion of the design and planning of environments, as well as the development of environments through spontaneous events in the classroom and outside as a response to children's interests and ideas. This chapter will typically raise questions about how we stimulate play with older learners and how we allow the element of choice within activities for the children.

To begin we need to revisit what the objectives are of the play that we wish to initiate with the children. The following is a good starting point for any adult beginning to plan for play. In Chapter 2 we outlined six roles for older learners playing and used these to form our play principles for primary aged children. These were:

- child as autonomous learner
- child as creative learner
- child as investigator
- child as problem solver
- child as reflective learner
- child as a social learner.

Additionally, in Chapter 5 the Croftlands Junior School case study showcased how the staff developed their own principles about their play-based approach to learning. Regardless of the play principles you adhere to yourself or in your school, what is crucial is that you are explicitly aware of these when you are planning. By subscribing to your principles, you are more effectively able to provide appropriate conditions for learning.

Making connections with the existing curriculum

This can be seen in two ways. Firstly, there is the existing curriculum from government and then secondly, the curriculum that may already have been planned within school. This partly reflects the first but is about more than merely ensuring that the curriculum is delivered; it is also about personalising or adapting to local needs via medium-and/or long-term planning. Whichever view of an existing curriculum you are taking there can be pressure to ensure that the children are given access to the expected curriculum. As discussed in Chapter 5, teachers can feel the pressures of the existing curriculum and the need to cover it, and are aware of external expectations. This can lead to the view that everything should be planned to ensure specific outcomes. A play-based approach to learning is flexible and therefore addresses children's needs and builds on their strengths (for more discussion of this see Chapter 8).

 Points for reflection

Consider the forthcoming curriculum you have planned for your class and which parts might lend themselves to the development of play activities. How would this approach enhance the learning of the curriculum? Which skills, knowledge and attitudes would play activities offer children the opportunity to practise or develop further?

In addition to considered planning of play opportunities there are also times when you may want to be freer in the planning you undertake. The following section explores this, acknowledging the tensions that exist and offering one possible solution.

Taking account of children's interests

Play is freely chosen, personally directed, intrinsically motivated behaviour that actively engages the child ... Play can be fun or serious. Through play children explore social, material and imaginary worlds and their relationship with them, elaborating all the while a flexible range of responses to the challenges they encounter. (National Playing Fields Association (NPFA), 2000: 6)

This is particularly a challenge for teachers of primary or elementary aged children with a curriculum to teach and, as discussed in the previous chapter, there are always concerns about coverage. However, a period of heavy snow might generate an interest in peoples who live in cold climates and how they construct their home using snow, for example. This could be built on by the teacher by allowing the class to construct an igloo in the classroom or outside using different modelling techniques to show scale and size of the home. Is there room in your own planning to build on serendipitous opportunities such as this? After all, we are reminded that many scientific discoveries were made through serendipitous learning (Spalding, 2000).

Tracking curriculum coverage

When using a play-based approach to learning, you will see children taking their learning beyond or away from the curriculum objectives you originally planned. Depending on your confidence and other external factors, you may encourage the children to pursue this or you may need to refocus the children back to your original intention. What is important is your own record keeping and how you maintain a record of what the children have learnt. This will be discussed further in Chapter 7 but is also a consideration in planning.

One effective way to track coverage of the curriculum in a play-based approach is to use the yearly objective tracking sheets that are used for individual children. By using only one for each subject, it is possible to list the objectives in the left-hand column and use the remaining columns to identify time periods during the year. As planning is carried out and as learning progresses, it is possible to make annotations about the extent to which the objectives are addressed generally by your class. Not only does this format provide a document for you to account for the children's learning you have planned and observed at a whole-class level, it also serves as a key document for planning further learning during the year as you can very easily identify gaps or areas for development. Crucially, it is a map for seeing where you have been as well as identifying possible direction of travel. See Figure 6.1 for an example.

Key learning experiences and activities

Mason and Johnson-Wilder note the difference between (mathematical) tasks and activity. They state:

Music Curriculum Coverage Tracking Sheet: 7-11 years of age

TERM / WEEKS / TOPIC	Controlling sounds through singing and playing – performing skills			Creating and developing musical ideas – composing skills		Responding and reviewing – appraising skills		
	1a sing songs, in unison and two parts, with clear diction, control of pitch, a sense of phrase and musical expression	1b play tuned and unturned instruments with control and rhythmic accuracy	1c practice, rehearse and present performances with an awareness of the audience	2a improvise, developing rhythmic and melodic material when performing	2b explore, choose, combine and organise musical ideas within musical structures	3a analyse and compare sounds	3b explore and explain their own ideas and feelings about music using movement, dance, expressive language and musical vocabulary	3c improve their own and others' work in relation to its intended effect
TERM 1 WKS 1-6 COLOUR				Representing 'colour' through composition (Also *)	Timbre			*
TERM 1 WKS 7-12 SACRED TEXTS	Hymns - one + two parts						Canons	
TERM 2 WKS 1-3 FRACTIONS	Musical notation (Also *)				*	Pitch + duration		

Figure 6.1 Tracking curriculum coverage example: Music

The purpose of a task is to initiate mathematically fruitful activity that leads to a transformation in what learners are sensitised to notice and competent to carry out. In learners' normal everyday activity, they initiate actions to satisfy their own motives, but educational activity is initiated in response to teachers' tasks. When a task is set, the *teacher's* intention is that the task will promote certain kinds of learning, but the *learner's* motive will depend on how the task is seen. (2006: 25)

Although we have already mentioned the dangers inherent in making all the decisions for children as this can lead to a lack of engagement with expected key learning activities, it is important to have thought about what might be possible key learning experiences that you want the children to gain. Depending on how confident you are within your planning and teaching, you may feel more secure in insisting the children meet particular outcomes. Alternatively, you may plan for these particular outcomes but allow the children to move away from these if it is appropriate. This rekindles the planning paradox (Ainley et al., 2006) introduced in Chapter 1.

It is important to distinguish between outcomes and outputs (Williams, 2011). Outcomes occur through activity whereas output is a tangible product. Often the process undertaken to produce an output has many more outcomes than the product itself shows. This is discussed further in the next chapter on assessing learning through play.

At the end of this chapter Table 6.1 provides a checklist you may find helpful when planning.

Children's involvement in developing the plans

Giving children choice and ownership over their own learning increases motivation and improves behaviour. It also impacts on the likelihood of them wanting to be involved in the future (Xiang et al., 2003). Starting with a 'what do we know and what do we want to find out?' lesson at the beginning of a unit or topic can spark children's imagination and motivation in a new play situation. Using an electronic poster tool such as 'Prezis', which is freely available for educational purposes, can be a very different way of producing linking ideas as part of the planning process. It is possible to track routes through the connected ideas, zooming in and out. This will assist children to choose resources to support the development of the environment. The more that the children are engaged in the overall design of the environment/activity, the more they are likely to remember and learn from the experiences. They are also developing their skills of problem solving and organisation as they work on planning, designing and resourcing the environment. In turn they are drawing on their creative, mathematical, historical, scientific, literacy and geographical skills which might be linked to any given environment.

Another way of gaining children's input could be to start with a resource, for example exploring the initial possibilities of plaster of Paris bandages or wire sculptures as one form of artistic play. Once the children have had a go with the resource then the class can discuss how an area might be developed so that children could explore the resources further. A visiting artist could also demonstrate some of the possibilities which the children can then replicate and/or develop to become their own ideas. We would argue for a co-construction of the play activities with the children informed by the curriculum, the interests and needs of the children as well as reflection upon previous experiences and assessments by the adults plus reflections on their own practice.

Creating the environment and providing the stimulus

Think about the case studies that you have already encountered in this book and consider the range of possible starting stimuli. For example, in Chapter 4 there was a book *The Friends of Emily Culpepper* which stimulated the villagers' meetings, and the playing at being a centurion in the Roman army was part of a topic about invaders and settlers.

There can be dangers in trying to impose pre-planned environments and activities on the children because of concerns about control. Baker-Sennett et al. (2008) discuss the differences between teachers who control and those who engage children in the process of planning. Their research found that not being directive resulted in better outcomes as the children naturally engaged with reading and writing activities as part of their play if they were not told that was what they had to do. As Anning suggests: 'It is unrealistic to argue that education contexts can offer the same freedoms to children's play behaviours as in the home or out of school settings/contexts' but she continues nor is it helpful to shape 'childrens' self-initiated play into a "sanitised" version for educational purposes' (2010: 29).

There can be occasions when the initial stimulus is very clearly planned but the activities that the children engage with and their use of resources is their choice. An example of this is the case study we met in Chapter 5. This can be seen in Baker-Sennett et al. (2008) when they differentiate between 'playplanning' and 'non-playplanning'.

> 'Non-playplanning' was play-related events that did not involve decisions about the play, such as reading a script provided by the adult, puppet making under the direction of the co-oper, rote rehearsals with no proposals for change, or imitating something already decided … Planning could occur 'in character' or 'out of character'. (2008: 1003)

They also argue that the children's involvement in planning assists the development of their own planning skills and the co-ordination of plans with others. The latter is a key skill for team work in later life.

The outdoors

When working with older primary or elementary aged children we can learn a lot from the work of early years practitioners and their relatively recent development of using the outdoors as an environment for learning. To begin with we want children to be aware of their surroundings indoors and out, and to look at environmental issues, citizenship and care for the local environment. There are concerns about children's engagement with their environment, as can be seen in the work of Thomas and Thompson when they say:

> Children are losing their connection with the natural environment and their wellbeing and environmental quality are inextricably linked. The worse a local environment looks, the less able children are to play freely … (2004: 3)

As a result of the lack of the use of outdoors for activities, with the exception of sport in many schools, children can initially view going outside as an excuse to run around and this can be coupled with Anning's concerns about 'the strategy of using "play outdoors" as a safety valve for boisterous, physical play for girls' and boys' (2010: 29). In order to ensure that children understand what going outside actually means during school time the adults need to prepare the ground rules carefully for the learners and also decide how this might be communicated to parents and carers, who may raise their own concerns about time spent outside the classroom.

Points for reflection

Some schools have small outdoor theatre spaces that can be used for dramatic play or there may be a natural bowl in the school grounds that might work as a kind of auditorium. If these kinds of spaces are available in your school then consider how to make more use of them for play of different kinds.

Planning for access for all

In planning environments consideration must be given to access for children with physical disabilities such as mobility issues or sensory impairment. All areas should be available to all children or variations made available in consultation with the children themselves to ensure that adults are not being even unintentionally patronising towards any child with any additional need. It can be easy to make assumptions that they might not cope with an area that has stairs, for example where the child may view this as a challenge or additional practice in managing that kind of environment. This is best negotiated directly with the children involved so they set the agenda and feel included rather than excluded from any of the decision making. You will also need to consider any cultural issues there might be with understanding the environment being created or specific issues about sensitivities to religious views.

Another way to provide access to all children might be to create an environment where everyone has their sight restricted, say with blindfolds, so that they must use their other senses more carefully to play in the environment. Sensory gardens work on a similar principle emphasising the sense of smell over the other senses, for example. Recreating a coal mine shaft with little light where children worked in dirty conditions could be a way of demonstrating what happens when you have limited sight in a cramped environment. More about play for all children is discussed in Chapter 8.

Differentiation

Differentiation is a necessary component to consider in all planning of learning opportunities. Pedagogical practice impacts on learner identity and social values (Raveaud, 2005) and therefore meeting children's needs through differentiation is as important in play environments as it is in other approaches to teaching and learning. If you plan for the play environment to offer an open-ended task then differentiation by outcome is possible. Managing differentiation through adult or child intervention is another valid approach. Sometimes planning to assign roles to specific children within an environment can challenge and extend their thinking. For example, 'What might you say in a given situation if you were in this person's shoes?' Asking children to research ideas, periods of history, scientific knowledge or other facts that they could use in a role play could provide extension work away from the play environment and inform their role development. Another form of differentiation by support is to consider the resources that are available to children (the use of resources is discussed further in the next section). Finally, peer support is a clear aid to differentiation when children are collaborating in mixed attainment groups during play-based activities.

Besides academic differentiation, your planning should consider other aspects of children's development and differentiate according to this if appropriate. For example, are there children in the class who need specific support when working with others? Who might you pair them up with? Or are you going to encourage them to select who they will work with? Does it matter whether they work with someone else or idependently?

Resources

Many theorists identify the need for children to use various resources and representations to support their learning (for example, Bruner, 1960, 1986; Dienes, 1969; Piaget, 1952; Skemp, 1987) and identify how resources can mediate social construction of knowledge (for example, Cobb, 1995; Vygotsky, 1978).

Collecting resources is a vital part of allowing children to choose and discuss what resources are the most appropriate for a given scenario. If you are not an early years practitioner it is worth visiting an early years setting to see the range of resources that they collect to support play environments. The resources need not be expensive as children can make things to sell in shops from clay, plasticine or junk. Drews explains how 'flexible uses of resources can encourage flexible thinking. This approach can help develop a classroom culture in which it is recognised that there are many paths to reach the same [destination]' (2007: 29).

You will need to think about storage when the resources are not being used and how they will be organised in the classroom. Also think about the extent to which you are going to allow the children to freely choose which resources they can use. For example, will children always have access to the internet, scrap paper or calculators? What limitations, if any, will you put on the resources and why? Turner and McCullouch suggest that allowing children a choice in the resources they use 'enhances the ability of children to apply their knowledge to new situation' (2004:65). Adults in the classroom are also resources – and the most expensive – so in your planning think about how this resource is going to be best utilised!

Thinking about adults' roles

Chapter 5 was dedicated to considering the roles that adults have in play-based approaches to learning, reflecting the importance of this aspect. Not only is it necessary to be aware of your role and the roles of other adults, it is also necessary to keep those roles in mind when you are planning. Will you encourage the other adults you are working with to adopt the role of manager as they organise the time, space and resources that promote play? Will they mediate, or interpret the play that occurs? Perhaps you will ask them to adopt an active role in the play, engaging in parallel play, co-playing or play tutoring (Dockett and Fleer, 2002).

Organisation and management of time

A key part of the planning and organisation is not just the location of the activities, environment or resources but when the children will be able to play in the space. You will need to decide when this occurs based upon your classroom or outdoor space and the organisation of the other activities when this occurs. You might decide that the activities will be available for the whole class every afternoon for a week or in the afternoon of one or two days in the week during the period of this particular project. Will all of the children be involved at the same time? Do all the children have to be involved at all? There are various ways you may group the children to be involved in play-based activities including:

- whole class
- attainment grouping
- self-selected groups
- interest groups
- pairs.

Teachers and trainees can be worried about letting children select their own groups. However, we have observed that when children are given the choice about who they may work with, they often look beyond friendship groupings to work with the most appropriate people for the task in hand. Of course this is often their friends, and what better way to encourage children to learn collaboratively than with children they have already developed highly sophisticated ways of relating to. Behaviour is also often more appropriate when children choose who they work with. Our observations concur with Boyatzis et al. who note using 'self-awareness, self-management, social awareness and social skills at appropriate times and ways in sufficient frequency to be effective in the situation' (2000: 3) shows emotional intelligence.

Reflection

Many teachers now have advanced skills in reflecting on their own teaching and on the children's learning. Afterall, Schön (1983) encourages teachers to take time to deliberately reflect through 'reflection on reflection in action', in order to develop a 'repertoire of knowledge and experience'. While it is important for teachers to reflect during evaluations of play experiences, we want to focus on planning for children to reflect on their own outcomes in a play situation. After all,

> Some have argued that play is children's work but I would say that it is far more than this. Play is their self-actualisation, a holistic exploration of who and what they are and know and of who and what they might become. (Broadhead, 2006: 89)

Supporting children in their ability to reflect upon how their thinking has changed is a critical part of a learning process (Hansen, 2008). Assessment for Learning (AfL) has led to a plethora of activities for helping children during their reflection process. It might be helpful when you are planning for children's reflection opportunities to use the materials provided on AfL websites and documents (for example, www.assessment-frform-group.org/index.html:www.aaia.org.uk/afl). Furthermore, plan for the children to reflect on two distinct parts of their involvement in the play activities.

1   What have you discovered?
2   What have you learnt?

The first relates to the 'hard' outcomes: what the children have found out. What declarative knowledge do they have now that they did not have prior to the activity? The second relates to the 'soft' outcomes: what they have learnt about their ability to carry out a particular task, their relationship with another child, assumptions they made about their own time management and so on.

Reflection on activities can often be reduced to writing about the activities that children have undertaken. Even this can have a very different feel with the use of technology, for example groups' blogs about the activities they have taken part in on a once a week basis over a half term. Robson's research looked at how 3–4-year-old children exhibited metacognitive behaviour. She found that there was a shift during an activity 'from a preoccupation with metacognitive skilfulness and planning and monitoring the activity ... towards more emphasis on displaying metacognitive knowledge in the children's later reflection upon it' (2010: 239).

Although we have presented 'reflection' towards the end of this chapter, be mindful during planning that opportunities for children to reflect are necessary throughout the play experience and should not only come at the end.

Bringing activities to a close, display and presentation

Rather than allowing the play environment to just become unused during the day or for the class to lose interest, it is important to consider how long an environment/activity will be available and how you will close the activity. One way is to have a culminating activity, such as a celebration. For example, the centurion soldiers returning home to their families and a traditional feast would mark the end of the activities linked to Roman soldiers and their way of life. It is then possible to start a new environment/activity which can be advertised ahead of time with a poster which proclaims what is coming soon.

Another powerful way to bring longer periods of play to a conclusion is to create a sense of audience for sharing the outcomes from the play. For example, displays of action photos could form a book, a wall display or a slide presentation on an IWB.

Beyond the wider school curriculum is the United Nations Convention on the Rights of the Child (UNCRC, 1989). In Article 12, point 1 states, 'the child who is capable of forming his or her own views [has] the right to express those freely in all matters affecting [them], the views of the child being given due weight in accordance with the age and maturity of the child'. This is followed up in Article 13 where 'the child shall have the right to freedom of expression; this right shall include freedom to seek, receive and impart information and ideas of all kinds, regardless of frontiers, either orally, in writing or in print, in the form of art, or through any other media of the child's choice'. By sharing findings with others children can feel empowered – which the convention states is their right.

Table 6.1 Checklist for planning

Have you considered?	Resources/issues	Tick/cross
Curriculum objectives		
Location of play environment		
Children's involvement in planning		
Inclusion issues		
Resources available for the children to use		
Trial activities with specific resources		
The overall design of the environment		
Time allocation: time each day, total time span for activities		
Behaviour expectations for the children		
Expectations for the adults of interactions and engagement		
Involvement of other expert adults		
Expected outcomes		
Communication with parents/carers		
Reflections by the children		
How you will assess skills, knowledge, attitudes		
How you will record any assessment		
How you will retain a record of the activities/environment		
How you will close the activities		
How you will evaluate the whole of the activities/environment		

Summary

This chapter has raised some challenges about planning for play activities with primary/elementary aged children. Consider the implications for your own practice by reflecting on the following questions.

1 What concerns do I have about planning for play?
2 How does my understanding of the concerns impact on my practice?
3 How can I give more control of the planning process to the children?
4 What changes might I need to make to my practice?
5 What are the benefits of play for children's learning?
6 What are the benefits for my teaching of using play approaches?

Further reading

Children's Play Council (2006) *Planning for Play: Guidance on the Development and Implementation of a Local Play Strategy*. National Children's Bureau/Big Lottery Fund. Available at: www.playengland.org.uk/resources/planning-for-play (accessed July 2011).

Drake, J. (2005) *Planning Children's Play and Learning in the Foundation Stage*. London: David Fulton.

Prezis details are available at: http://prezi.com/ (accessed July 2011).

Fogarty, R.J. and Pete, B.M. (2009) *How to Integrate the Curricula*. Thousand Oaks, CA: Corwin. Provides ten models of curriculum integration offering a way of addressing the issues of having to 'cover' curriculum objectives. All of the models they identify can be used in a play-based learning environment in primary schools and many address the issue of coverage.

References

Ainley, J., Pratt, D. and Hansen, A. (2006) 'Connecting engagement and focus in pedagogic task design', *British Educational Research Journal*, 32 (1): 23–38.

Anning, A. (2010) 'Play and legislated curriculum', in Moyles, J. (ed.) *The Excellence of Play*, 3rd edn. Maidenhead: Open University Press.

Baker-Sennett, J., Matusov, E. and Rogoff, B. (2008) 'Children's planning of classroom plays with adult or child direction', *Social Development*, 17 (4): 998–1018.

Boyatzis, R.E., Goleman, D. and Rhee, K.S. (2000) 'Clustering competence in emotional intelligence: insights from the Emotional Competency Inventory', in R. Bar-On and J. D. Parker (eds), *The Handbook of Emotional Intelligence:*

Theory, Development, Assessment, and Application at Home, School, and in the Workplace. San Francisco: Jossey-Bass. (pp. 343–62)

Broadhead, P. (2006) 'Developing an understanding of young children's learning through play: the place of observation, interaction and reflection', *British Educational Research Journal*, 32(2): 191–207.

Bruner, J.S. (1960) *The Process of Education*. Cambridge, MA: Harvard University Press.

Bruner, J.S. (1986) *Actual Minds, Possible Worlds*. Cambridge, MA: Harvard University Press.

Cobb, P. (1995) 'Cultural tools and mathematical learning: a case study', *Journal for Research in Mathematics Education*, 26 (4): 362–85.

Dienes, Z.P. (1969) *Building Up Mathematics*. London: Hutchinson Education.

Dockett, S. and Fleer, M. (2002) *Play and Pedagogy in Early Childhood: Bending the Rules*. Australia: Nelson.

Drews, D. (2007) 'Do resources really matter in primary mathematics teaching and learning?' in D. Drews and A. Hansen (eds.) *Using Resources to Support Mathematical Thinking: Primary and Early Years*. Exeter: Learning Matters Ltd. pp 19–31.

Hansen, A. (2008) *Children's geometric defining and a principled approach to task design*. Unpublished doctoral thesis. Institute of Education, University of Warwick. Available at: www.children-count.co.uk/images/PhD%20Final.pdf (accessed July 2011).

Hart, R. (2002) 'Containing children: some lessons on planning for play from New York City', *Environment and Urbanization*, 14 (2): 135–48.

Mason, J. and Johnson-Wilder, S. (2006) *Designing and Using Mathematical Tasks*. St Albans: Tarquin Publications.

National Playing Fields Association (NPFA), Children's Play Council and PLAYLINK (2000) *Best Play: What Play Provision Should Do for Children*. London: NPFA.

Piaget, J. (1952) *The Child's Conception of Number*. New York: Humanities Press.

Raveaud, M. (2005) 'Hares, tortoises and the social construction of the pupil: differentiated learning in French and English primary schools', *British Educational Research Journal*, 31 (4) 459–79.

Robson, S. (2010) 'Self-regulation and metacognition in young children's self-initiated play and reflective dialogue', *International Journal of Early Years Education*, 18 (3): 227–41.

Schön, D. A. (1983) *The Reflective Practitioner: How Professionals Think in Action*. New York: Basic Books.

Skemp, R.R. (1987) *The Psychology of Learning Mathematics*. Hillsdale, NJ: Erlbaum.

Spalding, E. (2000) 'Performance assessment and the new standards project: a story of serendipitous success', *Phi Delta Kappan*, 81 (10): 758–64.

Thomas, G. and Thompson, G. (2004) *A Child's Place: Why Environment Matters to Children*. London: Green Alliance/DEMOS.

Turner, S. and McCullouch, J. (2004) *Making Connections in Primary Mathematics*. London: David Fulton.

United Nations Convention on the Rights of the Child (UNCRC) (1989) 'Convention on the Rights of the Child'. Available at: www2.ohchr.org/english/law/crc.htm (accessed July 2011).

Vygotsky, L.S. (1978) *Mind in Society: The Development of Higher Psychological Processes*. Cambridge, MA: Harvard University Press.

Williams, H. (2011) Review Day at Croftlands Junior School, Ulverston. 12th May, 2011.

Xiang, P., McBride, R., Guan, J. and Solmon, M. (2003) 'Children's motivation in elementary physical education: an expectancy-value model of achievement choice', *Research Quarterly for Exercise and Sport*, 74, (1): pp. 25–35.

CHAPTER 7

ASSESSMENT OF PLAY-BASED APPROACHES TO LEARNING

Introduction

In this chapter we look at assessing and making judgements about what has actually been learnt during play activities for primary or elementary aged children. We will also explore how evidence of learning might be accessed, collected and evaluated, linking to more general materials about assessment.

A key question to ask is, 'Why might it be helpful for assessment of learning to take place?' We usually make assessments in order to:

- plan the next steps in learning and teaching
- give feedback to the learners to motivate them in the process of learning
- allow children to engage in a dialogue about their learning
- provide information for parents and carers about progress in learning
- evaluate teaching and resources including the learning spaces created.

 Points for reflection

Consider the five bullet points above about the purposes of assessment. To what extent are you:

- utilising assessment in your classroom or setting for these purposes?

(Continued)

(Continued)

- using both formative (assessment *for* learning) and summative (assessment *of* learning) for all these purposes?

  What could you do differently to ensure that you are fulfilling these purposes using formative and summative methods?

In addition to these pedagogical purposes, assessment is also used in England, Wales and several other countries to generate an accountability system for teachers. This political driver in raising standards is something that teachers are very mindful of when they are planning learning experiences for children and as a result children are 'being taught a limited and unbalanced curriculum, particularly but not exclusively in Year 6, as teachers feel constrained to tailor their teaching towards test preparation' (NUT et al., 2010: 3). We address this major issue in the next section.

Concerns about testing and its impact

> A system based on tests is flawed [because] ... it encourages methods of teaching that promote shallow and superficial learning rather than deep conceptual understanding. (ARG, 2006: 6–7)

We know from research (for example, Alexander, 2010; Assessment Reform Group, 2006; GTCE, 2011: 5; House of Commons Children, Schools and Families Committee, 2007–8; NUT et al., 2010: 3) and our own work with teachers that statutory testing at 11 years of age has a significant impact on the way teachers approach teaching throughout the primary school. The tide is shifting in relation to statutory national testing. For example, although the specifics vary, assessment reforms in Wales, Scotland and Northern Ireland have all led to reduced or no centralised testing and a marked increase in the reporting of teacher assessment (Assessment Reform Group, 2002). England appears to be following the trend, with more teacher control for assessment of children earlier in the primary age phase and with a large-scale assessment reform currently being undertaken (see www.education. gov.uk/ks2review).

Planning for assessment

Although testing remains a current issue, we wish to put this aside for the time being. After all, the Assessment Reform Group listed a number of reasons why an 'education system based on tests is flawed' (2006: 6–7). Among others, the first one listed is directly related to the reasons why we are encouraging a play-based approach and why we should look for reasons for supporting the children in our care to have high quality learning experiences:

> [Testing] fails to provide information about the full range of educational outcomes that are needed in a world of rapid social and technological change and therefore does not encourage the development of these skills. These outcomes include higher-order thinking skills, the ability to adapt to changing circumstances, the understanding of how to learn, and the ability to work and learn collaboratively in groups as well as independently. (2010: 6–7)

What is assessed?

There are many things that you will need to consider assessing as you plan for your assessment. These include the children's skills, knowledge, attitudes, interests, engagement and interactions.

In Chapter 5 the Croftlands Junior School case study provided a rare lens with which to critically engage with the issue of what to assess. One of the key issues for the teachers was what they could/should assess. The case study identified the following interrelated dichotomies:

- process/product: the children undertook a highly valuable process as they researched a topic of interest, but the end-product did not fully reflect their learning
- output/outcome: the end-product was simply an output of the children's activity and there were a significant number of high quality outcomes that were also evident through the project
- hard evidence/soft evidence: the project provided less 'hard' evidence (such as children's work output) than the teachers were used to but more 'soft' evidence (such as collaboration skills, researching skills, decision-making skills, empathy) than was normally evident in previous approaches to teaching and learning.

The staff are not alone. Research also identifies these difficulties. For example, Stokking et al. explain how 'the trend towards "soft" assessment adds complications of its own: assignments that involve options for topic choice by students can diminish the quality of the assessment between students' (2004: 95).

When, until very recently schools have been told 'most primary schools in the [mathematics inspection] survey had used the Primary National Strategy framework effectively to plan their mathematics curriculum' (Ofsted, 2008), it takes a very brave school to move away from these centrally driven guidance materials. But there is a growing shift in the way that schools are planning, teaching and assessing their own curriculum. For example, during the Cambridge Primary Review call for evidence, 'head teachers pointed out that exciting and creative lessons do more to advance basic skills than any narrow focus on them' (Alexander, 2010: 331–32).

 Activity

Choose one subject in the National Curriculum and scrutinise the learning objectives that you are statutorily obliged to address. Are they process-orientated or content-orientated? You may be surprised to find that many are process-driven and include such verbs as 'develop', 'use', 'generate ideas', 'understand' and so on. Although some objectives are content-driven, such as to learn 'that sounds travel away from sources, getting fainter as they do so' (DfEE and QCA, 2000), the vast majority are content-free such as 'talk about ... ideas'.

Now look at the assessment you have carried out for one medium-term plan for that subject. How much of the assessment is related to National Curriculum objectives and how much is related to objectives that you have made up yourself or that you have been given? We suggest that it is highly likely you are planning (and therefore assessing) far more objectives than you may need to.

Who is going to do the assessment – children and/or adults?

In Chapter 5 we looked at the importance of power in the play-based classroom and how it was essential to be aware of the impact that power has on children's motivation, behaviour and cognitive development. When we talk about teachers making decisions about children's attainment, the power is definitely held by the teacher. Equally, when the children have all the power and make decisions about their attainment, they may have a naive understanding of their attainment and the standards they are expected to attain. When considering the role of the teacher in relation to assessment, the fundamentals are not dissimilar to those discussed earlier in Chapter 5, particularly in relation to Dockett and Fleer's (1999) model of adult as player, adult as facilitator and adult as manager. However, as the play paradox discussed in Chapter 5 reminds us, ultimately teachers have a statutory obligation to support children in learning a set of prescribed objectives. As a result, the Assessment Reform Group suggests that:

> teachers should have clear criteria describing levels of progress in various aspects of achievement and, ideally, they should help to develop these criteria. As well as providing a common basis for interpretation of evidence, such criteria should also spell out the learning opportunities that are required. This makes it easier for teachers to assess pupils dependably on the basis of regular classroom work. (2010: 4)

Case study

This case study introduces us to Mel, a teacher who has worked with a range of children from 5–11 years of age. She reflects here upon her own experience of assessment through the eight years of her career.

'I started teaching ten years ago and I was Mrs Perfect when it came to my record keeping and my assessments. I remember having class tick lists with the objectives written down for every lesson, then I had group sheets I used to give to any other adults that worked with the children in the lesson. In the first few years I also experimented with sticky note pads where I wrote assessments down about children and I also had a clipboard permanently attached to my left arm! I thought I was doing well. I got lots of feedback from my induction tutor and head teacher, and parents who came into the class thought that I was the ideal teacher.

'When I became pregnant I left work and stayed at home for two years with Sammie. When I felt that it was right to return to work I got a job in a different school and off I set with my folders and files and exacting records. The head teacher had a very different approach to my previous head. My new head found me one day after school slaving over my class lists and he asked me a deceptively simple question: "Whose benefit is all that work for?" At first I was a little put out because I was used to impressing people with the paperwork. But I went home that night and thought about it a lot. And I realised that all that work had been benefiting my ego more than anything else. I was devastated! I wanted to be the best teacher I could be to help my children develop to the best of their abilities, and there I was focusing on what made me look good, rather than what was most effective.

'It took some time for me to learn how to do things differently, but I passed far more control over to the children – whatever age group I taught – and they rose to it. Sharing the responsibility for assessment with them not only made my life after school a lot more productive making sure more appropriate learning opportunities were available for the children, I even got home earlier! My husband and Sammie liked that change too!

'My advice for other teachers would be threefold. One, focus on what is important and decide if that has to be written down by the children, or an adult or if it can simply be mentally noted and acted upon. Two, ask the children what they have learnt and listen, listen, listen. So often I learnt what the children had really taken on board and it was so different to what their final output revealed. And third, give value to your own observations and what the children tell you. Not everything has to be written down to be evidence. High quality evidence comes from a number of avenues.'

Points for reflection

What do your assessments look like? Do you over-rely on children's completed tasks or are you competent assessing other 'soft' skills from discussion with children or observation? To what extent do you value children's assessments?

What methods of assessment will be used?

> Testing is frequently equated with assessment. This is a serious error – linguistically, technically and educationally. It ... diminishes the use of other kinds of assessment which have greater diagnostic and pedagogical value. Testing is just one kind of assessment among others. (Alexander 2010: 324)

Below is a list of assessment methods that you may be familiar with and/or use in your classroom. As can be seen from the list, there are a large number of methods that can be employed in a play-based approach to learning and each method has its own advantages and challenges. Several of the methods can be used formatively and summatively. When planning, ensure that a range of methods are used over periods of time. This is important because different children will have preferences for different assessment methods depending on their ability, demography, learning style and personality traits (Furnham et al., 2008).

Assessment methods include:

- children identifying what they have learnt and one thing they would like to learn more about
- learning representatives – one child from each table or group meeting with you to discuss their peers' opinions on the play activities on offer or being proposed
- children keeping a journal
- suggestion box – children posting comments for you to read
- assessment sheet for each child/pair/group to complete
- class discussion about learning through the play session(s)
- focused observations of individuals
- children marking each other's work, either leaving written comments or talking about the piece of work carried out
- children's reflections on their own learning process, asking questions such as 'What will I do differently next time?'
- passing around a large envelope and asking children to place one question or comment about the content of the lesson into the envelope for you to read later
- assessment dice: children taking turns to roll the dice that has the following six statements (or alternatives) that require a response that is then discussed further

  - What I found the hardest to do
  - One thing I found out
  - Someone who helped me
  - Next time I would like to ...
  - I practised ...
  - I am most proud about ...

- pinning a sheet of paper with a question, comment or learning objective written at the top for children to self-select their inclusion in the group later in the week. For example, 'I want to know more about how to create line graphs'
- children writing a letter to the teacher or another appropriate person about what they have learnt, or the process they have gone through
- group presentation or poster sharing findings
- peers critically feeding back their observations about the way children worked in a group or on a task
- reviewing a video or photos of children engaged in activity
- two children discussing their learning on 'hotseats' in front of the class or a group
- 'jigsawing' where children move around groups, discussing with the other members what they have learnt.

 Activity

As you read the list above make a note of the advantages in using each method. Also identify what some of the challenges may be. If appropriate, state what could be done to overcome the challenges. Finally, identify those methods that you are confident to use and which ones you would like to try out.

How is any evidence to be recorded and in what format?

Written assessment evidence

The case study above shows that not all assessments need to be evidenced. However, as well as the outputs from the above list, written records by adults and children can include:

- learning journeys
- diaries
- annotated work
- activities completed by the children
- topic webs (one colour before and another colour after the play-based approach has been used).

Although there are many written forms of assessment, just as valid – and often *more* valid – are other sources of evidence such as observation notes, which are discussed further below. Feeling confident in your assessment in a play-based approach to learning is important. It may take you some time to feel your assessment evidence is an appropriate alternative to traditionally accepted forms of formal recording.

Observation assessment evidence

In the early years assessment through play is predominately carried out through observation and when working with primary aged children this approach would also dominate. This doesn't include only watching what children do but also listening closely to what they say. Just observing sounds as though it would be an easy task but it requires adults to think carefully about what they have seen. Are the observers expecting specific behaviours to occur and therefore only looking for those? Does the absence of behaviours indicate a lack of understanding on the part of the child or is it linked to the choices they are making? A skilled observer manages to notice what is going on and is able to decide upon its significance. It can be easy to miss the behaviours and responses that indicate learning has taken place; practising is the only way to learn.

There are different kinds of observation that adults can use that allow the collection of different kinds of information. For example, a narrative of the observation may capture much of what is happening in the order it occurs, providing you with a broad sweep of activities in the classroom. If you are interested in specific interactions between individuals you might wish to develop a schedule that allows the collection of numbers of interactions between children and the actions involved.

It can be helpful to use a schedule to focus your observations and Table 7.1 is an example of one way to organise this.

Table 7.2 is a more focused observation on what occurred. If focusing on the adult activity, the record can be used for evaluation and if focusing on the children's activity, it can focus on assessment.

Or you may find that a less structured schedule is sufficient for your assessment of the children involved and Table 7.3 is just one example.

Remember that you may also find it useful to link to issues of inclusion and records of social interactions and not only learning outcomes.

Table 7.1 Example of a schedule to focus observations

Description of the context	Behaviours observed
<ul><li>Description of the area of provision, e.g. role play</li><li>Information about the children involved (e.g. number, age, sex) Is this a new activity for the children or one they are very familiar with?</li><li>Focus of the activity – subject and skills and knowledge focus</li><li>What do the adults do and say?</li><li>What do the children do and say?</li><li>How does the adult monitor the children's achievements? How are the children given feedback on their achievements?</li><li>Additional information, e.g. how long did the activity last? What did the children do next? What did the adults do next?</li></ul>	This can be a running record of what is happening. <ul><li>Child interactions (non-verbal and verbal)<ul><li>With self</li><li>With others</li></ul></li><li>Actions including drawing, writing and any other recording included in the activity</li></ul>

Table 7.2 Example of a schedule of a more focused observation

Entry to the session

Adult activity	Child activity
How do any adults welcome and direct the children?	How does the child know what is available?
Are there routine 'beginning' processes?	Does the child choose the activity or is the child directed?
How is the session set out to facilitate the start?	
Resources used?	Evidence of child's interest and motivation?
What does the teacher or other group leader do to direct children?	Does the child interact with other children?
	What vocabulary does the child use?
What do adults do to engage children?	What resources does the child use?
Questioning? Listening?	What is the level of the child's independence?
What do the adults do if a child is not engaged in an activity?	
	Is there a product such as a drawing, writing, model?
What is the balance of adult to child talk?	
What areas of learning do the activities address?	What happens to this child's 'work'?

Self-selected activity

Adult activity	Child activity
How do adults direct the children to any choices that they can make?	How does the child know what is available?
Are there routine 'beginning' processes for chosen activities, such as getting an apron, putting on outdoor shoes, etc.?	Does the child choose the activity or is the child directed?
	Evidence of child's interest and motivation?
How is the session set out to facilitate the start?	Does the child interact with other children?
How is the space set out to facilitate choice?	What vocabulary does the child use?
Where are the adults based?	What resources does the child use?
What do the adults in the setting do?	What is the level of the child's independence?
What do adults do to engage children?	
Questioning? Listening?	Is there a product such as a drawing, writing, model?
What do adults do if a child is not engaged in an activity?	
	What happens to this child's 'work'?
What is the balance of adult to child talk?	How long does the child stay working in one area/on one activity?
What areas of learning do the activities address?	

Session conclusion

Adult activity	Child activity
How do the adults conclude the session?	What signal do the children respond to in this part of the session?
What learning do the adults revisit?	
What feedback is given to the class/groups/individuals?	How do the children clear away/return apparatus and material?
Do any of the children report back on what they have done?	Are the children willing to present work/ideas?
Do the children know how well they have done? Or how well they have behaved?	Are the children willing to reflect upon their learning?
Are new targets/challenges set?	
How long does this part of the session last?	
How do the adults manage any transitions?	
What evidence do the adults have that learning has been achieved?	
How does the teacher dismiss the class/group?	

Table 7.3 Example of a less structured schedule

Date	Observer	Children involved in play activity
Context		
Learning outcomes planned		
Notes from observation		
Learning outcomes achieved (these may be different from those planned)		
Targets and next steps for learning		
Review		

Other assessment evidence

Johnson suggests that play 'not only reflects or is a window on child development but also contributes to it both by consolidating or reinforcing recent learning and conceptual acquisitions and by providing opportunities for new masteries and novel insights' (1990: 214). As a result it is important to consider a wide range of assessment evidence to inform your insights into how the children in your care are progressing. Other sources of evidence might include:

- e-portfolios
- online discussions on VLEs
- feedback from parents
- self and peer reflections
- pictures/photographs
- audio
- video.

You may also decide to put aside time during play sessions to discuss assessments with children. After all, assessment should be an integral part of learning and not something that is tacked on. Talking with children about their learning and assessment decisions that have been made (by you or them) can positively impact upon the children's attainment and their understanding of standards (Koshy, 2009).

Assessing social play

For children who have specific difficulties with social interactions, which might include children with an autistic spectrum disorder (ASD) or those with anger management issues, it is important to make judgements about progress in this area. Keeping a record of who they play with, when and how can be helpful in planning the next steps in their social learning. An example of what you might record follows in Figure 7.1.

Date	Observer	Focus child
	Context	
	Learning outcomes planned	
	Notes from observation	
	Interactions initiated by target child	
	Note who the child approached and how the approach was received	
	Interactions responded to by target child	
	Note who approached the target child and how the approach was received	
	Learning outcomes achieved (these may be different from those planned)	
	Targets and next steps for learning	
	Issues for grouping target child for other learning activities	
	Review and discussion with parents/carers	

Figure 7.1 Example of a record of progress for children who have difficulties with social interactions

Reporting assessments

Another aspect to consider when planning for assessment is with whom this information is shared and how it is shared with children, other adults working in the school and parents/carers, and the purpose in sharing it. This will also have an impact on the detail and the quality of any recording that is done. If the assessment is for a wider audience, you may keep more detailed records. Again, we can take the head teacher's question in the earlier case study 'Whose benefit is all that work for?' and assess, record and report accordingly.

At times it can be difficult to communicate with parents or carers about children's attainment. Using a range of mechanisms for communicating that go beyond the statutory formal school reports reflects the more flexible ways that a play-based approach to learning embraces. Additionally, communicating with parents or carers is more than simply reporting a summative assessment; it is about enhancing learning (Green and Oates, 2009).

 Case study

In this case study we meet Lawrence, 13 years old, who is reflecting on his 'best' teacher at primary school and why he held that opinion.

'I was nine but I was new at the school 'cos I went to live with my Aunt. You see my Mum was more bothered with her new man than me. I wasn't bothered about school, I liked my Nintendo and that was about it. But my teacher, Mrs E, she was alright actually. The other kids really respected her and although I had been expelled from my last school for throwing a chair at my last teacher I thought I'd give her a go. The big difference was that she listened to me. No one else had done that before. She spoke to me about what I did [in lessons] and why I did it. She was impressed with my way of thinking about things and she'd ask me to take the lead on some things and she didn't mind if I couldn't do something. Near the end I used to go straight up and tell her when I was not getting it and she would just smile at me. Everyone else had always shouted at me to get back to my seat or to shut up.

'But it didn't stop there. She sent notes home to my Aunt and they were always about something good I'd done. At first I didn't show them to my Aunt cos, well, I was too embarrassed I guess. I had an image to keep up, man, and it wasn't right to tell her anything at school, ey. But Mrs E saw through that and she phoned my Aunt instead. That was even more embarrassing at first but then Mrs E said the three of us should sit down and talk about what I was doing in school. I wasn't perfect by any means 'cos I had problems with my anger management like I still do, but it felt good to get out of my old town and start again. I owe a lot to Mrs E for getting me positive about school and including my aunt in it.'

As can be seen in the case study above, communicating with parents/carers can be key to a child's development and success in school. What might be less obvious is the impact that *not* communicating with a parent/carer can also have.

Feedback to parents/carers does not need to be as time consuming as the case study above may suggest. For example, giving a younger child a sticker encourages discussion at home about the reasons for being given the sticker. Another simple but highly effective way to communicate with parents/carers is to have on hand a stock of small slips or cards that provide information about certain aspects that are important to you. Some examples are given in Figure 7.2.

Dear Mr and Mrs Stephenson

Just a note to let you know that **Sara** was superb in the group work that she did today.

I especially liked the way that s/he **spoke clearly and made great eye contact in her group presentation** and I thought you'd like to know too!

Best wishes
Mrs Stone

Dear Mum

Just a note to let you know that Ollie blew us all away today with the way he was so kind to the new child in our class!

Kind Regards
Miss Vaukins

Magical Maths Moments

Today, _Simon_ was an amazing mathemagian because _he used his data-handling skills in science very well!_

S/he'd love to tell you all about it!

Figure 7.2   Samples of school-to-home notes

☐ **Summary**

Play allows opportunities for adults working with primary aged children to see how they make use of the knowledge, skills and attributes learnt within subject learning in a more relaxed setting. It offers opportunities for dialogue about what they have learnt and for the children to showcase the connections they are making within and between subjects. It will also allow access to children's misconceptions which may not be obvious in other approaches to assessment. This links to the child as a reflective learner. Consider the implications for your own practice by reflecting on the following questions.

1 What concerns do I have about assessing play?
2 How does my understanding of the concerns impact on my practice?
3 How can I give more control of the assessment process to the children?
4 What changes might I need to make to my practice?
5 What are the benefits of assessing children's learning through play-based activities?
6 What are benefits for planning my teaching of using assessment information from play-based activities?

Further reading

Bew, P. (2011) *Review of Key Stage 2 Testing, Assessment and Accountability: Progress Report.* Available at: https://media.education.gov.uk/MediaFiles/8/6/8/%7B868C26F0-986E-43AF-A6E7-424BF2C72592%7DKS2Review%20Final%20040411%20progress%20report.pdf (accessed July 2011).

Klugman, E. and Smilansky, S. (eds) (1990) *Children's Play and Learning.* New York: Teachers College Press.

References

Alexander, R. (ed.) (2010) *Children, their World, their Education: Final Report and Recommendations of the Cambridge Primary Review*. London: Routledge.

Assessment Reform Group (2002) *Principles of Assessment for Learning: 10 Principles*. Cambridge: University of Cambridge, Faculty of Education.

Assessment Reform Group (2006) 'The role of teachers in the assessment of learning'. Newcastle Document Services. Available at: www.assessment-reform-group. org/ASF%20booklet%20English.pdf (accessed July 2011).

Department for Education and Employment (DfEE) and Qualifications and Curriculum Authority (QCA) (2000) *The National Curriculum Handbook for Primary Teachers in England Key Stages 1 and 2*. London: Stationery Office Books.

Dockett, S. and Fleer, M. (1999) *Play and Pedagogy in Early Childhood*. Marrickville NSW: Harcourt Brace.

Furnham, A., Christopher, A., Garwood, J. and Martin, N.G. (2008) 'Ability, demography, learning style, and personality trait correlates of student preference for assessment method', *Educational Psychology*, 28 (1): 15–27.

General Teaching Council for England (2011) *Department for Education (DfE): Key Stage 2 Testing and Accountability Review. Response from the General Teaching Council for England*. London: GTCE. Available at: www.gtce.org.uk/documents/publicationpdfs/dfe_ks2testing0211.pdf (accessed July 2011).

Green, S. and Oates, T. (2009) 'Considering alternatives to national assessment arrangements in England: possibilities and opportunities', *Educational Research*, 51 (2): 229–45.

House of Commons Children, Schools and Families Committee: Testing and Assessment, Third Report of Session 2007–8. Available at: www.publications. parliament.uk/pa/cm200708/cmselect/cmchilsch/169/169.pdf (accessed July 2011).

Johnson, J.E. (1990) 'The role of play in cognitive development', in E. Klugman and S. Smilansky (eds), *Children's Play and Learning*. New York: Teachers College Press. pp. 213–34.

National Union of Teachers, Association of Teachers and Lecturers and the National Association of Head teachers (2010) *Common Ground on Assessment and Accountability in Primary Schools*. London: The Strategy and Communications Department of The National Union of Teachers.

Koshy, S. (2009) 'Using marking criteria to improve learning: an evaluation of student perceptions', *Journal of Systematic, Cybernetics and Informatics*, 7 (1): 72–76.

Ofsted (2008) *Mathematics: Understanding the Score*. London: Ofsted. Available at: http://www.ofsted.gov.uk/Ofsted-home/Publications-and-research/Browse-all-by/Documents-by-type/Thematic-reports/Mathematics-understanding-the-score (accessed July 2011).

Stokking, K., van der Schaaf, M., Jaspers, J. and Erkens, G. (2004) 'Teachers' assessment of students' research skills', *British Educational Research Journal*, (1): 93–116.

CHAPTER 8

INCLUDING ALL LEARNERS IN PLAY

An entitlement to learning must be an entitlement for all pupils ... to ensure that all pupils have a chance to succeed, whatever their individual needs and the potential barriers to learning might be. (DfES/QCA 1999: 3)

Introduction

This chapter will explore the issue of making play accessible for all learners in primary or elementary education regardless of any specific additional needs they might have which need to be taken into account. In doing so we do not go into detail about specific needs; instead we discuss a number of generic considerations that apply to most children at any time. We would argue that by adopting a play-based approach the issues of access for the adults to deal with are lessened as the types of activities reduce some of the issues and can positively promote inclusive practices. Inclusive practice is not just about working with the children but it includes all adults, parents, carers and families right from the planning stage (Erkins and Grimes, 2009). Everyone needs to feel included in all aspects of practice with opportunities for discussion and feedback at all stages to avoid misunderstandings and creating barriers to participation.

This chapter on inclusion focuses on two of our key play principles: the child as a reflective learner and the child as a social learner. Speaking and listening is clearly a central activity for a social learner and this will be linked to role play and the needs of children for whom English is not their first language. We will be focusing not just on language skills acquisition but also on subject knowledge learning as both are important.

What do we mean by inclusion?

The following quotation from Alison John from Kidsactive and the Better Play Awards sums up the issue:

> Inclusive play provision is open and accessible to all and takes positive action in removing disabling barriers so that disabled children and non-disabled children can participate. (cited in Children's Play Council, 2006: 14)

Inclusion is the availability of opportunity for *all* learners to experience and learn from activities through the removal of any barriers to learning. These may be physical, emotional, social, cultural, religious or cognitive. These aspects are addressed by the global movement towards a policy of 'personalised learning' where there has been 'a shift in the root-metaphor of schooling from transmission to construction' (Beach and Dovemark, 2009: 690). The Teaching and Learning in 2020 Review Group addresses what it interprets 'personalised learning' to mean. We see this as encompassing a pedagogical approach that is addressed by the discussion in this book.

> Close attention is paid to learners' knowledge, skills, understanding and attitudes. Learning is connected to what they already know (including outside the classroom). Teaching enthuses pupils and engages their interest in learning: it identifies, explores and corrects misconceptions. Learners are active and curious: they create their own hypotheses, ask their own questions, coach one another, set goals for themselves, monitor their progress and experiment with ideas for taking risks, knowing that mistakes and 'being stuck' are part of learning. Work is sufficiently varied and challenging to maintain their engagement but not so difficult as to discourage them. This engagement allows learners of all abilities to succeed, and it avoids the disaffection and attention-seeking that give rise to problems with behaviour. (Teaching and Learning in 2020 Review Group, 2006: 6)

Removing the barriers

Some barriers can be removed through discussion with the specific children involved. For example, making a den for children to play in the classroom and having a child who is a wheelchair user means considering either making the entrance to the den large enough to accommodate the wheelchair or having a separate entrance that can be closed after the child has entered the den to preserve the dark environment. Spencer-Cavaliere and Watkinson's (2010) research findings offer an insight into the perspectives of children with disabilities.

They interviewed eleven 8–12-year-old children with a range of disabilities (including cerebral palsy, fine and gross motor delays, developmental co-ordination disorder, muscular dystrophy, nemaline myopathy, brachial plexus injury and severe asthma) about their perspectives on inclusion in play-based activity. What was most important to the children was the actions of others thus that allowed them to gain entry to play, feeling like a legitimate participant and having friends. Allowing children with additional needs to say how they would like access to environments and listening to how they would like things to work is an important step towards inclusive practice.

Speaking and listening as part of being an effective reflective and social learner

Any activity that encourages communication can support the needs of all learners but can be particularly helpful for children with any language and/or communication additional needs as they give a purpose to the interactions. Quiet children can sometimes get lost in a busy, noisy classroom and get overlooked. Collins (1996) highlights the issue of this group of children in her book *The Quiet Child*. Her research work came from her frustration with this group as they appeared to exhibit behaviour which actively discouraged communication including rarely speaking in class and being reluctant to ask for assistance if difficulties arose. Collins links this to not being able to listen carefully to these children. This work was written before the emphasis from the Primary Strategies on more focused whole teaching yet even in this situation children developed strategies to avoid communication. We would argue that a play approach offers these children an opportunity to engage in different ways and provides space for adults to be able to listen to children more carefully. Working in small groups assists these quiet children to develop their confidence in speaking and listening in ways that whole class interactions do not. The case study of Emily Culpepper in Chapter 3 of the villagers' meeting included children who we would identify in this quiet category yet they could participate in the meetings first through listening and hearing how others might model discussions before feeling confident to volunteer their own contribution.

As adults we appear to want to insist that everyone contributes in the same way but we are happy to acknowledge that adult learners may prefer to listen rather than to actively contribute. Can we not give children the same freedom of opportunity? Providing they contribute at some point during the term we perhaps shouldn't be insisting that everyone contributes all the time. We want social learners but we want *confident* social learners who have thinking space before deciding whether or not to contribute rather than contributing for the sake of just having something to say. This is a difficult balancing act to achieve for all learners.

The following review of research provides a short case study of children with EAL who often as a result of their lack of linguistic skills and confidence fall into the 'quiet child' category.

The impact of play situations on children with EAL

A recent study by Grant and Mistry focused on the use of role play in a class of 8–9-year-olds. They raised the question, 'If language acquisition is thought to benefit from the use of role-play, would it not be beneficial for EAL pupils to participate in such activities, designed to enhance the acquisition of aural and oral skills?' (2010: 155). They acknowledge that there has been little specific research about role play with EAL children in Key Stage 2 settings though they found one study in Bradford suggested that with multi-lingual children 'role play had proved very successful in generating powerful talk' (Conteh et al., 2006: 58). There were also studies that looked at role play as a 'time filler' (Harrison et al., 2005) and at the underuse of the play (van Ments, 1983). Cast argued that role-play areas need not only be used with children from 3–7 years old but with older primary/elementary learners as role-play activities can provide '… a wealth of learning experiences' higher up the age range, allowing children to explore everyday activities with freedom' (2007: 22). Grant and Mistry's research asked three key questions:

1   Are there any language, cultural or religious considerations to be taken into account when planning a role-play activity?
2   Will language prove to be a barrier for some EAL children undertaking a role-play activity, allowing others to dominate the lesson at their expense?
3   Can the use of role-play aid the recall of vocabulary at a later date, or is its worth merely transitory? (2010: 156)

The setting for their research was a class of 8–9-year-olds within an urban, multicultural school in which the majority of the children spoke two or more languages and most were Urdu and Punjabi speakers. They chose two groups of children to work with: the first they covertly observed during the lessons and the second were observed overtly with participation with a focus on role play.

The results of the observations raise key questions for practitioners who work in a multicultural environment. Children from this cultural heritage talked to adults in a different way, appearing shy and sometimes refraining from making eye contact because of the cultural norms of their society. There was also a need for translation where appropriate to avoid any misunderstandings or misconceptions. This emphasises the need for understanding about cultural differences to avoid placing children in a position of conflicting behavioural expectations.

Able linguists as you might expect dominated the role play and less able linguists used body language, gestures and facial expression to assist them in gaining access to the activities. The implications of this for teachers centred around how they might group children to engage with role play activities, selecting the less able linguists to work together with adult support so they would benefit from direct modelling from adult interaction and would not be disengaged through being overwhelmed by the more competent linguists.

Although Grant and Mistry (2010) found that the interactions increased over time with the use of role play the results in relation to the use of vocabulary proved inconclusive, though there appeared to be marked improvement in the children's use of technical language. They conclude their paper with the following quotation: 'The research undertaken has shown that role-play activities can have a positive effect on the learning of EAL children, by encouraging interaction and providing a means of assimilating vocabulary in a pressure-free context' (2010: 162). They suggest teachers consider the grouping of children for role-play activities as any mixed ability grouping allows for social interaction and peer modelling, whereas the use of bilingual or adult support can encourage specific language learning, especially technical classroom vocabulary. How a teacher might decide to group the children in the class is dependent upon the intended learning outcomes of the activities and based upon knowledge of linguistic and social factors.

Roles for children with additional needs more generally

Although the case study above focuses on EAL children, there are communication and social interaction issues for many children with additional needs. Role play can support them in learning how to interact with others. Table 7.4 in Chapter 7 provides an observation schedule that could be used to evaluate the impact of role play for specific children and assess their interaction skills.

 Points for reflection

Other research concurs with the findings of this research project. For example, Chen and Li identified that 'meaningful vocabulary learning occurs only when the learning process is integrated with social, cultural and life contexts' (2010: 341). Consider how you might group your current class for role play after reading this research project. You may not have any EAL children but you are likely to have some children who are quieter than others. Think about children who might dominate the speaking and perhaps not listen as closely. Identify the skills that you want to enhance through role play as this will assist in thinking about appropriate groupings. Are there opportunities to enhance children's reflective learner skills by thinking about how they contribute to activities and how they allow others to engage effectively?

Cultural barriers removed?

When working with children from a range of cultural backgrounds it can be an oversight to see all educational practice just from a western perspective. Children's social learning concerns relationships with others and the extent to which they feel competent and related, as stated by Wentzel:

> The social worlds of children are a pervasive and influential part of their lives at school. Each day in class, children work to maintain and establish interpersonal relationships, they strive to develop social identities and a sense of belonging-ness, they observe and model social skills and standards of performance displayed by others, and they are rewarded for behaving in ways that are valued by teachers and peers. (1996: 1)

It is important that practitioners are aware of differences in behaviour patterns and the underlying potential reasons for their occurrence. As adults we need to respect cultural norms that might cause discomfort to children if asked to act in specific roles. These can be simple things like not showing the sole of your foot to someone as it is considered impolite or more complex patterns of behaviour. When we use play as a medium for learning we need to:

1 Move beyond Western theories of play for analysing play
2 Note the range of expression of pretend play evident across cultures
3 Determine the value play has for particular cultural groups prior to planning
4 Develop programs which recognise and support different cultural or multi-cultural approaches to play
5 Observe play in terms of culture and gender and desconstruct interactional patterns together with children and their families to ensure equity for all children. (Fleer, 1997, cited in Dockett and Fleer, 2002: 129)

When using play activities it is advisable to discuss the activities with the children and parents and carers as part of the planning process. This is likely to avoid difficulties or misunderstandings, particularly in relation to social, cultural and religious issues that might arise. It gives all parties an opportunity to become involved and no one feels excluded from the start. Allowing children access to experience things outside their own cultural backgrounds also develops their understanding of other cultures, further assisting them to become effective reflective and social learners. The interest and motivation of children from different cultural groups and the extent to which adults or children direct play-based learning opportunities can assist adults in thinking about the balance of play activities and how to engage all children right from the start.

Lillemyr et al. (2011) found in their studies in the US, Australia and Norway that in all countries a significant tendency was found for indigenous groups (Aboriginal Australian, Navajo Indian, Sa´mi) of children to be more strongly interested in directed activities compared with non-indigenous groups. Their focus was on play generally and in the US and Australia there were limited opportunities for children to play in the class with the exception of mathematics games. All children felt play was important for them both in and out of the classroom and some of the children in the study from indigenous groups felt they would actually learn better through more play activities despite a preference for adult directed activities and a more traditional view of education. This impression appears to be signalled from the majority culture. For this reason, it seems indigenous children expect learning in school to be teacher directed, in contrast to the free learning at home.

In the discussion section of their paper Lillemyr et al. suggest that they:

> … have seen that even 8–10-year-olds have a strong need for free play, showing the potential of play in school learning, not the least when taking into account play's dimensions of intrinsic motivation and social interaction. In play, children interact with others and build social competence, providing them with useful experiences and the potential for creativity, experimentation, and learning strategies. (2011: 57)

They go on to argue for more free play or free learning opportunities for this age group which further supports our autonomous learner through play. Lillemyr et al.'s (2011) study also supports adults working with primary aged children from different cultural backgrounds to enhance the quality of engagement and learning in play activities in the classroom.

The following is a case study that started from a child-initiated idea but involved the whole school.

 Case study: Planning an African market

In a large 7–11 school that was very involved in charity fund raising several of the children suggested finding out more about markets in different parts of Africa. Each class chose a country to research and find something they could make or purchase to sell at the African market. They researched the languages spoken and tried to access a few simple phrases. Each class had a market stall space in the school hall so they could sell their wares. To begin with they designed and built a space that reflected the culture of the country and displayed things you might find as an advertising space for their stall. Figure 8.1 shows one of the stalls as the children began to develop this space in the hall to illustrate their chosen country, in this case Ethiopia. The children chose how they wanted to work together and how they wanted their space to look. Although there was actually no one in the local community from Ethiopia this class found out as much as they could to inform potential shoppers at the market.

(Continued)

(Continued)

Figure 8.1 One class chose an Ethiopian market stall

When all the classes were ready the market was open for the whole school, parents/carers and the rest of the local community. Each stall was staffed by a rotation of children from the associated class who told people what they had learnt and explained the wares for sale. At this point it was clear from the way in which the children spoke accurately about their chosen countries that they had gained a substantial amount of knowledge about the countries. There was also evidence of understanding of the cultural differences in the language they used to describe how people lived, for example. They were no longer making assumptions about living conditions but were able to discuss the practical issues in relation to keeping animals safe by having them with the people in their houses. Proceeds from the sales were sent to the Save the Children charity.

 Points for reflection

What kinds of approaches do you use to communicate with parents/carers and the wider community about activities carried out in school? How inclusive is this? Which groups are not well represented? How might a different form of communication reach this/these group(s) and help to engage them in the school community? Is it possible to plan play activities around a cultural theme with assistance from the local communities such as a market like the one in the case study above that would engage people from the planning stage through to the closure and evaluation? Could the children make choices about the focus, research and ways of working which would enhance their skills as autonomous, investigative, social and creative learners?

Class barriers removed?

Another barrier that is widely researched and documented is social class. Government policy for the personalised learning agenda in England and Wales claims to link personalised learning and social justice (DfES, 2004) or social mobility (Miliband, 2003). However, critical commentators such as Burton (2007) question this as theoretical and political rhetoric. Additionally Harris and Ranson (2005) identify contradictions in the linking of these two agendas.

Furthermore, researchers (for example, Beach and Dovemark, 2005, in Sweden; Campbell et al. 2007 in England) have questioned how theoretical policy-driven play-based approaches to learning can address social barriers in practice. Campbell et al. remind us that:

> personalisation is a collective activity, not an individualised one, but the collective frame leads to the individual developing her/his learning ... It is also collective in another sense; the values and attitudes that teachers and students bring to learning is derived from, and embedded in, a collective organisational ethos. (2007: 151)

Indeed, in his keynote address to the National Union of Teachers (NUT) National Education Conference in 2004, Professor Robin Alexander states:

> I shall argue that *personalisation* and *choice* – today's buzzwords and tomorrow's inevitable election manifesto pledges – are meaningless without a generous concept of entitlement, and especially without a proper curricular and pedagogical foundation at the foundation stage and Key Stages 1, 2 and 3. In June 2004, Liberal Democrat leader Charles Kennedy argued that good local schools for *all*, not choice between good and poor schools, should be the Government's priority, especially if schools rather than the parents do the choosing. (2004: 16)

Alexander's concerns may be well founded. One finding from Beach and Dovemark's (2005) research related directly to the impact that social class may have on the way that children are equipped to engage in play-based learning opportunities and the way that teachers respond to children from different social backgrounds. In their 18-month longitudinal Swedish study, they identified that teachers valued some children's choices more highly than others' and found, therefore, that 'existing social and cultural hierarchies are reproduced and stabilised rather than challenged or overturned by/in the practices we have documented and by/inside the logic of these practices' (2005: 701).

Martin Johnson from the Institute for Public Policy Research identifies similar potential issues and calls for a change in existing practice.

In a world of increasing geographical mobility and cultural mixing, the work of schools in producing cohesion within mixed communities becomes ever more important. In a world of increasing anomie, the work of schools in producing shared community values replaces cultural production by religions in earlier times. Would we be in need of Anti-Social Behaviour orders if schools had been recognised and supported in this work over the last two decades? From this perspective, to call for the personalisation of education is to demand the intensification of a process which has already gone too far. Rather, progressives should call for the socialisation of education. Schools should be enabled to emphasise and support the collective in social life as a balance against the individualistic. They should be encouraged to offer shared learning experiences, not individualised ones. (2004: 224)

 Summary

This chapter has focused on inclusive practices in relation to play activities. Consider the implications for your own practice when building inclusive play activities by reflecting on the following questions.

1 How engaged are all learners?
2 What are the barriers for specific groups/individuals to accessing play activities?
3 What adaptations might need to be made to activities to allow access for all?
4 How might I group children to work in play environments to support learning?
5 How might teaching support assist specific children's engagement with activities?
6 How might we celebrate and learn from the cultural diversity in the class/ school?
7 What links with the wider community might play activities help to foster?

Further reading

Collins, J. (1996) *The Quiet Child*. London: Continuum International Publishing.
Knowles, G. (ed.) (2006) *Supporting Inclusive Practice*. London: David Fulton Publishers.

References

Alexander, R. (2004) 'Excellence, Enjoyment and Personalised Learning: a True Foundation for Choice?', keynote address to the National Union of Teachers (NUT) National Education Conference, 3 July 2004. Available at: www.robinalexander.org.uk/docs/NUT Educ Review 2004 article.pdf (accessed July 2011).

Beach, D. and Dovemark, M. (2005) 'Creativity as a cultural commodity: An ethnonographic investigation of struggles over creativity in three Swedish schools', *Journal for Critical Education Policy Studies*, 4(2). Availabel at: www.iceps.com (accessed July 2001).

Beach and Dovemark (2009) 'Making "right" choices? An ethnographic account of creativity, performativity and personalised learning policy, concepts and practices', *Oxford Review of Education*, 35 (6): 689–704.

Burton, D. (2007) 'Psycho-pedagogy and personalised learning', *Journal of Education for Teaching*, 33 (1): 5–17.

Campbell, R.J., Robinson, W., Neelands, J., Hewston, R. and Mazzoli, L. (2007) 'Personalised learning: ambiguities in theory and practice', *British Journal of Educational Studies*, 55 (2): 135–54.

Cast, J. (2007) 'Role-play in Key Stage 2', *English 4–11*, 29: 22.

Chen, C-M. and Li, Yi-L. (2010) 'Personalised context-aware ubiquitous learning system for supporting effective English vocabulary learning', *Interactive Learning Environments*, 18 (4): 341–64.

Children's Play Council (2006) *Planning for Play: Guidance on the Development and Implementation of a Local Play Strategy*. National Children's Bureau/Big Lottery Fund. Available at: www.playengland.org.uk/resources/planning-for-play (accessed July 2011).

Collins, J. (1996) *The Quiet Child*. London: Continuum International Publishing.

Conteh, J., Davids, S. and Bownass, K. (2006) 'Talking, learning and moving on to writing', in J. Conteh (ed.), *Promoting Learning for Bilingual Pupils 3–11: Opening Doors to Success*. London: Paul Chapman Publishing. pp. 42–62.

DfES/QCA (1999) *The National Curriculum: Handbook for Primary Teachers in England KS 1 and KS 2*. London: DfES/QCA.

Department for Education and Skills (DfES) (2004) *A National Conversation about Personalised Learning*. Nottingham: DfES.

Dockett, S. and Fleer, M. (2002) *Play and Pedagogy in Early Childhood: Bending the Rules*. Australia: Nelson.

Erkins, A. and Grimes, P. (2009) *Inclusion: Developing an Effective Whole School Approach*. Berkshire: Open University Press.

Grant, K. and Mistry, M.T. (2010) 'How does the use of role-play affect the learning of Year 4 children in a predominately EAL class?', *Education 3–13*, 38 (2): 155–64.

Harris, A. and Ranson, S. (2005) 'The contradictions of education policy: disadvantage and achievement', *British Educational Research Journal*, 31 (5): 571–88.

Harrison, L., Robins, J., Cartledge, F. and Meiner, J. (2005) 'Remaking role-play in Barnsley', *English 4–11*, 25: 18–20.

Johnson, M. (2004) 'Personalised learning: new direction for schools?' *New Economy*, 11 (4): 224–28.

Lillemyr, O.F., Sobstad, F., Marder, K. and Flowerday, T. (2011) 'A multicultural perspective on play and learning in primary school', *International Journal of Early Childhood*, 43 (1): 43–65.

Miliband, D. (2003) 'Opportunity for all: targeting disadvantage through personalised learning', *New Economy*, 10 (4): 224–29.

Spencer-Cavaliere, N. and Watkinson, E.J. (2010) 'Inclusion understood from the perspectives of children with disability', *Adapted Physical Activity Quarterly*, 27 (4): 275–93.

Teaching and Learning in 2020 Review Group (2006) *2020 Vision: Report of the Teaching and Learning in 2020 Review Group*. London: DfES. Available at: www. education.gov.uk/publication/eOrderingDownload/6856-DfES-Teachingand%20 Learning.pdf (accessed July 2011).

Van Ments, M. (1983) *The Effective use of Role-play: A Handbook for Teachers and Trainers*. London: Croom Helm.

Wentzel, K.R. (1996) 'Social goals and social relationships as motivators of school adjustment', in J. Juvonen and K.R. Wentzel (eds), *Social Motivation: Understanding Children's School Adjustment*. New York: Cambridge University Press. pp. 226–47.

CHAPTER 9

TRANSITION TO SECONDARY SCHOOL

Introduction

The transition from primary to secondary school is well documented in the literature as a significant time in children's lives (Pratt and George, 2005) and should not be underestimated given that it is 'one of the most difficult in pupils' educational careers' (Zeedyk et al., 2003: 67). We have found that one of the reasons some teachers feel that a play-based approach is less appropriate for children who will enter secondary schooling in the next few years is because the teachers feel they have to 'prepare' children for this transition and life beyond. This chapter has been written in an attempt to dispel this myth.

This chapter focuses on two aspects of transition to secondary or post-11 education. We are advocating that in the liaison and transition between the two phases of education the important issue is to build upon the knowledge and skills established in the primary/elementary phase when children transfer to secondary schools. The first area is the issue of how the knowledge and skills built up through a play approach to learning can be used in a secondary subject focused curriculum. The second is related to liaison and joint working between primary/elementary and secondary schools. To illustrate this a case study shows what might be possible when different phases of education work together on a play-related project.

Transitions of knowledge and skills to secondary school

There is significant research identifying the groups of children who may be more affected by transition from primary to secondary school, for example, lower ability (Anderson et al., 2000; Chedzoy and Burden, 2005), sociodemographic factors (Galton et al., 2000), gender (Anderson et al., 2000; McGee et al. 2003), socioeconomic factors (Anderson et al., 2000; McGee et al., 2003), ethnicity (Graham and Hill, 2003) and so on. However, by focusing on the different roles for the learners we have advocated throughout this book, we believe that it is possible to focus on children's skills, capabilities, learning dispositions, aptitudes and interests through transition and to develop a positive period of transition for children regardless of the 'group' in which they may placed. As a reminder we list the roles again for you here:

- child as autonomous learner
- child as creative learner
- child as investigator
- child as problem solver
- child as reflective learner
- child as a social learner.

However, the National Foundation for Educational Research's report prepared for the Northern Ireland Council for the Curriculum, Examinations and Assessment about the transition from primary to secondary education in Australia, Finland, Germany, Japan, the Netherlands, New Zealand, Singapore, Spain and Sweden (Le Métais, 2003) showed how the reporting from primary schools to secondary schools does not necessarily relate to these aspects of play-based approaches.

> School reports generally indicate how students have performed in each of the subject areas and, in some cases, comment on other aspects of student behaviour and attitudes. Whilst we can assume that this covers 'knowledge and understanding', the extent to which it also reports on 'skills and personal capabilities' and 'dispositions to learning, aptitudes and interests' is less clear, and may vary between schools or even between teachers. (Le Métais, 2003: 7)

Consistency and quality of transition paperwork

A concern about the quality of the information passed on about transferring pupils was also raised by Williams (2003) in the *Times Educational Supplement*. She identified that some large secondary schools could have in excess of 30 feeder schools and wondered if this was a cause. However, Ofsted (2008: 17) found that there was no link between the quality of transition arrangements and the number of feeder schools. Ofsted did identify that secondary schools in a particular area rarely agreed on transition protocols and this complicated matters of induction for primary schools.

Additionally Ofsted raised an issue about the extent to which secondary schools use the documentation given to them, finding that secondary schools 'failed to ensure effective continuity or progression in individual subjects' (2008: 17) from the last year in primary school to the first year in secondary school. Jones found that 'repetition and discontinuity in teaching and learning from one year to the next serves to demotivate pupils ... as the new work underestimates what they are capable of doing and achieving' (2010: 176). This seems to have a profound effect on children's progression. Indeed, Williams (2003) noted that a range of research papers from the last twenty years, using standardised testing as a measure, have identified that 20 per cent of pupils fail to make progress in English, reading and mathematics by the end of their first year in secondary school.

These issues are illustrated in the following case study where Steve, a secondary school art teacher, talks about his experiences of receiving children from a range of primary schools into his school. Furthermore he identifies the issues that arise because of the range of experiences the children from the various feeder schools have had and how the school audits children's art skills when they enter the secondary school.

 ### Case study: Building on children's primary school experience at secondary school

'When the children are in their first year of secondary school, their skills are disparate. This is due to their previous experience and not their ability. We try to address this by providing support to the teachers of our feeder schools. They need a balanced curriculum because for some children it is their lifeline.

'There is an issue with the National Curriculum and working towards statutory testing. I find that some primary teachers do not feel comfortable with "mess", or they don't have the skills required to deliver, or they think that art is expensive, or perhaps even "what is the point of art?"

'Children need an all-round education. Art is just as important as everywhere else. We have students here who struggle with maths and English, but put them on the stage and they blossom. We identify that talent and harness it. We give them support and opportunities. Effective transition is so important.

(Continued)

(Continued)

'Because the children's experiences are really varied in primary school when they first come we give them a baseline assessment. That gives them an opportunity to look at drawing, colour mixing and general awareness in art. We give them a National Curriculum level. We don't set but it gives us somewhere to start. The level is useful because it informs teaching and focus in schemes. We look for an upward trend with levels and if that is not happening we address that.'

The first part of this chapter has raised a number of issues about what information is passed from primary to secondary schools and how that information is used. The next section, about joint working, may offer one solution for primary schools, although we acknowledge the complexity of primary schools feeding into several if not many secondary schools.

A look at transition through a play-based lens

In a unique longitudinal research study following over 2000 Scottish pupils from 10/11 to 18/19 years of age, West et al. (2010) were able to pinpoint how a successful transition was critical for later well-being and attainment. They found that half of all children recalled being anxious to some extent about coping with the start of secondary school, with another quarter finding the experience 'very difficult' (2010: 44). Of all these children, there were more concerns expressed about the formal secondary school system than the informal system of peer relations. Furthermore, West et al. found that primary schools had more impact when preparing children for school issues than coping with peers. By following a play-based approach several outcomes can be harnessed by a receiving secondary school. The types of outcomes that are possible (Bell, 2010) include:

- greater understanding of a topic
- deeper learning
- higher-level reading
- increased motivation to learn
- independent thinking
- designing inquiries
- planning learning
- organising research
- implementing a multitude of learning strategies.

Jones (2010) looked at how AfL could be embedded into practice in MFL teaching in the last year of primary school and the first year of secondary school in order to support children's transition. She found through child narratives that 'a cross-phase conversation between teachers needs to include how to build on pupils' learning skills and engage pupils as active agents in the process of progressing their own learning' (2010: 175). As the case studies throughout this book demonstrate, play-based approaches to learning develop these skills. By focusing on outcomes such as those listed above, children may feel more confident about learning in a secondary school setting where those types of outcomes are certainly expected.

 Points for reflection

In the case study earlier in this chapter Steve mentioned his willingness to work with staff from feeder primary schools. What opportunities and barriers could be present in developing joint continuing professional development (CPD)?

Joint working

Capel et al. (2007) researched the transfer of pupils from primary to secondary school using a case study approach of a foundation subject: physical education. They identified how primary and secondary teachers must have a shared understanding and use of terminology and the National Curriculum levels.

One such approach to developing this shared understanding is CPD, led by specialist secondary staff and supporting primary staff. Although previous research (Williams, 1997, cited in Capel et al. 2007) found that this approach is motivating to staff and children and enhanced primary teachers' teaching, Capel et al. (2007) identified two potential problems with this model of working.

1   Secondary specialists may not have the expertise to cover the full range of development needed across the full primary range.
2   Secondary specialists' expertise may not be welcomed by primary colleagues.

Capel et al.'s research found that 'to establish trust and respect for one another as professional practitioners requires time to nurture and to build effective working relationships' (2007: 27). The case study below visits Dallas Road Community Primary School, Lancaster, which marked its centenary with a week of celebrations including painting an outdoor mural. The project involved collaboration between representatives from each class at Dallas Road, Year 11 (15–16-year-old) students on a creative and media diploma course from Central Lancaster High School (CLHS) and a graffiti artist. It demonstrates the opportunities that come from positive relationships between schools.

Case study: A centenary mural

The process

Communication between Dallas Road and CLHS: Agreement to work in collaboration to produce the mural and to jointly fund the graffiti artist.

Selection of one art representative per class: Older children applied using the child-friendly role description provided and were selected by their teacher.

Briefings in each school: Dallas Road children led their class through a process where each class put forward a design for the mural; CLHS students planned workshops to run with Dallas Road art reps.

Workshops: CLHS students led two workshops which included providing information about the graffiti artist, discussing class proposals and identifying what represented the school.

Final proposals: CLHS students worked with the graffiti artist to create three final designs. These were presented to the Dallas Road art reps who discussed and made final amendments to the preferred design.

Mural day: The graffiti artist worked with the reps and CLHS students to plan out and install the mural.

To tell us more about the project, working with others, and the impact on those involved we hear from Sara Bradley, the Dallas Road art co-ordinator, Victoria O'Farrell, Assistant Head Teacher at Central Lancaster High School, a 6-year-old child involved in the project, who we shall call Libby, and her mother, Janine.

Celebrating a centenary of the school (Sara Bradley)

'We wanted to mark the school with an everlasting stamp. We wanted to celebrate it through art that everyone can see. We have a number of links with partners such as Central Lancaster High School. We want the children to know about community cohesion and that it doesn't just happen in school but also in other areas of the community. We want to give them as many opportunities as are available to be inspirational and aspirational. We're making as many links with other groups as possible because it is beneficial to the children.

'[The project] raised the profile of art. The children see cool art on the wall and learn that art can take many forms. During the workshop the reps found it hard to use words in the art. They learnt a lot about logo work and graphic design and using the computer for art. They explored representation and symbols. The day also encompassed numeracy because they were using their bodies to measure. It was also challenging for them to use a vertical canvas as they were used to being able to grab their paper and manipulate it but this was a solid wall. Many gained in confidence.

'You hear the other children around the school say "that's my football" because the ideas represented the school. It gives all the children a stronger sense of community and belonging. All the children saw the mural being developed throughout the day. There is a buzz around the school about art.

'Going into the future we will keep art reps. Their job will be promoting art throughout the school, commenting on art in school, giving feedback on displays, getting ideas from their class on what they would like to do. We will keep working with partnerships. They learn from other children, adults and from meeting more people.'

Involvement of secondary students (Victoria O'Farrell)

'We are a Specialist School in Visual and Performing Arts. We have a commitment to work in the arts with six primary schools and Dallas Road is one of them. The mural project involved Year 11 students on the Creative and Media Diploma course. The students wanted to work together on making a collaborative piece of public art. They wanted to create something that would "lift peoples" hearts.

'The students planned and resourced two workshops. The first was about what are they proud of about school. [The Dallas Road children] talked about diversity, success, art, PE and other key curriculum areas, games and fun. They discussed the whole school and not just about it being somewhere you go to learn.

'The Year 11s developed their team work, planning, resources, time management, taking on leadership roles, researching, artistic skills. When they were at Dallas Road I was bowled over by them; they confidently took the lead and they were amazing at the delivery of the workshops. They gave words of encouragement rather than doing the drawings and designs for them. It was wonderful to see. They developed their awareness of others and how to support and assist others.'

A 6-year-old child's perspective (Libby)

'It was weird at first because it didn't look much like a mural. It looked like a white thing with circles and squares with crosses in them. They were for the school logo and the sun. Then it started looking like a picture. My favourite part was me painting. I kept getting it on my fingers. I painted for all of the morning and half the afternoon. It was fun cos I was watched by lots of people. We liked

(Continued)

(Continued)

celebrating that our school is one hundred years old. That's why we painted the mural. It is going to stay there for ever and ever and ever.'

A mother's perspective (Janine)

'They were the best days going to school. Libby felt incredibly proud to be the art representative. She used to come home walking tall. [Through the process] she felt like she was really being listened to. She wanted to find out what a mural was. [At home] she looked at [local artist] Chas Jacob's mural of the school [www.dallasroad.lancs.sch.uk/index.php?category_id=7]. She wanted to paint her own. She worked on it for seven nights and looked at everything and was so particular about what was going on.

'[On the day] she was up early and she got everything ready the night before. She came home and said that it was all really interesting and not a single part of

Figure 9.1 Libby's contribution to the mural

Figure 9.2 The finished mural

(Continued)

the day was boring. A couple of weeks later she was watching a CBeebies pro-gramme and the presenter said "We're all artists" and she replied "I know I am an artist". I said "What do you mean?" and she said "I know I'm an artist because I painted the mural at school".

'This could be her strength and that has been the positive for her and for us. It is nice to find that at her age. Quite often you don't know. She has had to be focused and we're hoping that focusing will transfer to other areas.'

Using a play-based approach in primary and secondary school

The case study above demonstrates how the children's roles and types of play we introduced in Chapters 2 and 3 have impacted on the primary children, secondary students and the wider primary school community including parents. Libby was *being* an artist through replication play. The roles she

Table 9.1 Play-based approaches to learning in the primary and secondary school

Learner's role	Types of play	Activities at primary	Activities at secondary
Child as reflective, social and investigative learner	Role play/ social dramatic play	Taking part in a history lesson about being a Roman soldier	Taking part in a history lesson about being a young person working in a mill during the late 1800s
Child as autonomous investigator and problem solver	Replication and exploratory	Science problem-solving activities where the child is in the role of scientist	Similarly, secondary age students are set activities where they must be autonomous learners, not always individually but in groups, to problem solve and take on the role of scientist investigating specific situations
Child as creative and social learner	Role play/ social dramatic play	Circle time/personal social and emotional development	Students in drama and life skills are asked to take on specific roles working through situations where conflict may arise e.g. playing a parent whose child has come home late and how they might handle this situation – his gives students an opportunity to explore their own and other feelings in specific circumstances
Child as social, reflective and problem solver	Replication and role play	History role play	Running simulations of elections so that students begin to understand their role as electors of the future, either related to life skills and/or history
Child as creative, problem solver	Virtual play	Website design	Website design

undertook included being autonomous (by representing her class as an art rep), creative (selecting designs to represent the school), a problem solver (making decisions), and social (leading class discussions, working with the art reps and with the high school students), while being involved in a reflective process.

A significant reason for ensuring effective transition is to support children's development in their move from primary to secondary school. The case study demonstrated how building on skills developed in play-based approaches to learning can be a natural progression in secondary school. Table 9.1 brings together the children's roles and the types of play with examples of play across the two age groups demonstrating how the skills learnt in one phase of education can be and are used with much older learners.

Most of the examples focus on the arts subjects of English, drama, history and life skills with only one focusing on science as the arts initially appear to be a more natural link for the transfer of knowledge and skills from primary/elementary to secondary school.

How play might support the transition with engagement in science, technology, engineering and mathematics (STEM) subjects

Once learners enter the secondary phase of education the specialisation of subjects can often mean that learning becomes compartmentalised. At the same time learners' engagement with specific subjects can shift as attitudes about learning knowledge and skills alter. The STEM areas are traditionally the most challenging for teachers to engage students in learning and then choosing to continue beyond compulsory age into related careers (Galton et al., 1999). Perhaps electronic play will help to address some of these wider issues. Archer et al. (2010) have begun a longitudinal study about students' engagement with school science. They identify how, at the age of 10, children often display a positive attitude towards science, but only four years later their interest seems to have declined. It appears that there is a barrier between 'doing science' and translating this into 'being a scientist'. Archer et al. suggest that

> the main issue at stake here is the potential to construct and inhabit an intelligible science identity – one that is valued in and for itself, that is congruent with other aspects of a person's identity, and that is also (seen to be) judged by others as being of worth. (2010: 628)

By using exploratory play as a pedagogical approach, we suggest that the disjuncture Archer et al. have identified can be avoided or narrowed because the children do not pretend to be scientists, rather they are scientists. To read more about being a scientist, see the section in Chapter 3 about replication play.

Points for reflection

When you have the next liaison meeting between primary and secondary phases, is it possible to find out more about the activities in each phase that could provide a progression of skills, knowledge and experiences across the education system? What more might be planned and utilised in both phases of learning that could support the development of this strand of learning more effectively?

 Summary

In this chapter we have looked at two different aspects of transitions. The first is about working together on projects to build up skills from both ends of the age phase. The second is to try and identify activities that are already undertaken that develop this way of working and how this ensures progression in skills, knowledge and experiences.

1 What kinds of play-based activities might it be possible for you to consider working on with your local secondary school?
2 What benefits for both schools can you see not just in terms of liaison but in relation to promoting different ways of working?
3 How could you see joint working in this way supporting children's transition to secondary school?

Further reading

DfES (2003) *Excellence and Enjoyment: A Strategy for Primary Schools.* Nottingham: DfES Publications.

DfES (2006) *Seamless Transitions – Supporting Continuity in Young Children's Learning.* Norwich: DfES. This is a support pack including a DVD for schools and early years settings.

DCSF (2008) *Strengthening Transfers and Transitions: Partnerships for Progress.* Department for Children, Schools and Families.

Powell, R., Smith, R. Jones, G. and Reakes, A. (2006) *Transition from Primary to Secondary School: Current Arrangements and Good Practice in Wales.* Final Report. Slough: NFER.

Turnball, A. (2006) *Children's Transitions: A Literature Review.* Cambridge: Cambridgeshire's Children's Fund.

References

Anderson, L.W., Jacobs, J., Schramm, S. and Splittgerber, F. (2000) 'School transitions: beginning of the end or a new beginning?', *International Journal of Educational Research,* 33: 325–39.

Archer, L., Dewitt, J., Osborne, J., Dillon, J., Willis, B. and Wong, B. (2010) '"Doing" science versus "being" a scientist: examining 10/11-year-old schoolchildren's constructions of science through the lens of identity', *Science Education*, 94 (4): 617–39.

Bell, S. (2010) 'Project-based learning for the 21st century: skills for the future', *The Clearing House*, 83: 39–43.

Capel, S., Zwozdiak-Myers, P. and Lawrence, J. (2007) 'The transfer of pupils from primary to secondary school. A case study of a foundation subject – physical education', *Research in Education*, 77: 14–30.

Chedzoy, S.M. and Burden, R.L. (2005) 'Assessing student attitudes to primary–secondary school transfer', *Research in Education*, 74: 22–35.

Galton, M., Gray, J. and Ruddock, J. (1999) *The Impact of School Transitions and Transfers on Pupil Progress and Attainment*. London: HMSO. Available at: www.suffolk.gov.uk/NR/rdonlyres/F13D257F-3034-4A93-AC09-5554080E73AC/0/PupilPerformanceResearchAnnex21.pdf (accessed July 2011).

Galton, M., Morrison, I. and Pell, T. (2000) 'Transfer and transition in English schools: reviewing the evidence', *International Journal of Educational Research*, 33: 340–63.

Graham, C., and Hill, M. (2003) 'Negotiating the transition to secondary school', *Spotlight 89*. The SCRE Centre, University of Glasgow.

Jones, J. (2010) 'The role of Assessment for Learning in the management of primary to secondary transition: implications for language teachers', *Language Learning Journal*, 38 (2): 175–191.

Le Métais, J. (2003) 'Transition from Primary to Secondary Education in Selected Countries of the INCA Website'. London: NfER Available at: www.inca.org.uk/pdf/probe_secondary_selected.pdf (accessed July 2011).

McGee, C., Ward, R., Gibbons, J. and Harlow, A. (2003) *Transition to Secondary School: A Literature Review. A Report to the Ministry of Education*. Hamilton: University of Waikato, New Zealand.

Ofsted (2008) Evaluation of the primary and secondary national strategies 2005–07. Available at: http://www.ofsted.gov.uk/Ofsted-home/Publications-and-research/Browse-all-by/Documents-by-type/Thematic-reports/Evaluation-of-the-Primary-and-Secondary-National-Strategies/(language)/eng-GB (accessed July 2011).

Pratt, S. and George R. (2005) 'Transferring friendships: girls' and boys' friendships in the transition from primary to secondary school', *Children and Society*, 19: 16–26.

West, P., Sweeting, H. and Young, R. (2010) 'Transition matters: pupils' experiences of the primary–secondary school transition in the West of Scotland and consequences for well-being and attainment', *Research Papers in Education*, 25 (1): 21–50.

Williams, E. (2003) 'Primary/secondary transition'. Available at: www.tes.co.uk/article.aspx?storycode=380390 (accessed July 2011).

Zeedyk, S., Gallacher, J., Henderson, M., Hope, G., Husband, B. and Lindsay, K. (2003) 'Negotiating the transition from primary to secondary school: Perceptions of pupils, parents and teachers', *School Psychology International*, 24 (1): 67–79.

INDEX

TEACHING CHILDREN 3 – 11

A Student's Guide

Third Edition

Editedb y **Anne D Cockburn** *University of East Angliaa* nd **GrahamH andscomb** *Essex County Council*

Focusing on the major topics underpinning professional studies strands in primary and early years teacher education, Teaching Children 3-11 provides indispensable coverage of vital practical and conceptual issues that support good teaching practice. This third edition of the popular textbook has been carefully revised following detailed lecturer feedback to meet the evolving needs of students training to teach across the 3-11 age range.

Featuring four new chapters on curriculum development, cross-curricular teaching, diversity and inclusion, and communication in the classroom, and engaging with the growing need for Masters-level study in teacher education, the new edition offers a balanced contemporary overview of modern teaching practice in an engaging and accessible manner.

This is essential reading for all students on primary and early years initial teacher education courses including undergraduate (BEd, BA with QTS), postgraduate (PGCE, SCITT), and employment-based routes into teaching. It will also be invaluable for those starting out on their professional careers.

CONTENTS

November 2011 • 368 pages
Cloth (978-0-85702-486-2) • £70.00 / Paper (978-085702-487-9) • £23.99

ALSO AVAILABLE FROM SAGE

CREATIVITY IN THE PRIMARY CLASSROOM

JulietD esailly *Education Consultant*

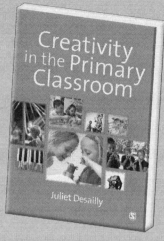

'This book deepens and broadens our understandings of creativity as applied to primary education. It provides a balance of practical frameworks and approaches with wise guidance. Many schools and individual teachers will find Juliet Desailly's work invaluable as they embrace the greater pedagogical and curricular freedoms promised by government.' - *Jonathan Barnes, Senior lecturer in Primary Education at Canterbury Christ Church University.*

Creativity is an integral element of any primary classroom. It has been never more important for teachers to involve children in their own learning and provide a curriculum that motivates and engages. Being creative involves generating new ideas, reflecting upon and evaluating different teaching approaches, and establishing an environment that supports creativity.

Creativity in the Primary Classroom explores how to develop as a creative teacher and how to foster creativity in your classes. Drawing from key literature and detailed real-life examples, Juliet Desailly puts into practice her extensive experience planning, advising and developing creative approaches to teaching and curriculum planning.

This book examines what creativity in a primary classroom can look like, and is supported throughout by practical activities for use across curriculum subjects and reflective tasks encouraging critical engagement with key conceptual issues.

This is essential reading for students on primary initial teacher education courses including undergraduate (BEd, BA with QTS), postgraduate (PGCE, SCITT), and employment-based routes into teaching, and also for practicing teachers wishing to enhance their own teaching.

CONTENTS

Section One: What is Creativity? \ The Key Elements of Creativity \ Creativity in Education: History and Theoretical Background \ PART TWO: A CREATIVE CHILD IN A CREATIVE CLASSROOM \ Building the Skills to Work Creatively \ Establishing the Ethos \ PART THREE: A CREATIVE TEACHER \ What Makes a Creative Teacher? \ Key Skills for the Creative Teacher \ PART FOUR: A CREATIVE CURRICULUM \ Planning for Creative Outcomes \ Medium Term Planning for Creative Outcomes \ Case Studies: Creativity in Practice

READERSHIP

This is essential reading for Students on primary initial teacher education courses, as well as practicing teachers wishing to enhance their own teaching

March 2012 • 176 pages
Cloth (978-0-85702-763-4) • £60.00 / Paper (978-0-85702-764-1) • £19.99

PROFESSIONAL STUDIES IN PRIMARY EDUCATION

Editedb y **HilaryC ooper** *University of Cumbria*

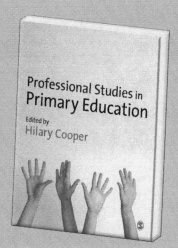

Developing an understanding of the professional aspects of teaching is an integral part of training to teach in primary education, and requires a broad and deep engagement with a wide number of practical and theoretical issues.

Professional Studies in Primary Education provides a wide-ranging overview of everything you will need to know to prepare you for your primary initial teacher education course, and your early career in the classroom.

Covering practical issues including behaviour management and classroom organisation, through to thought-provoking topics such as reflecting on your own teaching practice and developing critical thinking skills in the classroom, this textbook offers a modern and insightful exploration of the realities of teaching in primary education today. This approach is supported by:

- An awareness of current policy developments and statutory requirements
- Examining complex, multi-faceted issues in education
- Exploring alternative approaches to primary teaching practice
- Investigating ways to encourage personal and professional development as a teacher
- A companion website which includes extended essays adding further context to chapter content

This is essential reading for all students on primary initial teacher education courses including undergraduate (BEd, BA with QTS), postgraduate (PGCE, SCITT), and employment-based routes into teaching.

CONTENTS

PART ONE: INTRODUCTION TO PROFESSIONAL STUDIES \ **Susan Shaw** History of Education \ **Hilary Cooper** Philosophy of Education and Theories of Learning \ **Suzanne Lowe and Kim Harris** Planning, Monitoring, Assessment and Recording \ **Jan Ashbridge and Jo Josephidou** Classroom Organization and the Learning Environment \ **Jan Ashbridge and Joanne Josephidou** The Role of the Adults \ PART TWO: INCLUSIVE DIMENSIONS OF PROFESSIONAL STUDIES \ **Lin Savage and Anne Renwick** Reflective Practice in the Early Years: A Focus on Issues Related to Teaching Reception-Age Children \ **Verna Kilburn and Karen Mills** Inclusion and Special Educational Needs \ **Deborah Seward** Behaviour Management \ **Verna Kilburn and Karen Mills** Personal and Social Development \ **Donna Hurford and Christopher Rowley** Dialogical Enquiry and Participatory Approaches to Learning \ **Diane Warner and Sally Elton-Chalcroft** Race and Ethnicity: Teachers and Children \ PART THREE \ **Andrew Read** Reflective Practice \ **Diane Vaukins** Enquiry and Critical Thinking \ PART FOUR \ **Andrew Slater** Exploring Educational Issues \ **Nerina Diaz** Statutory Professional Responsibilities \ **Hilary Cooper** Moving into Newly Qualified Teacher Status

August 2011 • 272 pages
Cloth (978-0-85702-733-7) • £65.00 / Paper (978-0-85702-738-2) • £20.99 /
Electronic (978-1-4462-4989-5) • £20.99

ALSO AVAILABLE FROM SAGE

Made in the USA
Middletown, DE
12 August 2016